LIVERPOOL FC
Official Yearbook 2000

GRANADA
MEDIA

Written and Edited by John Keith
Statistics Compiled by Dave Ball and Ged Rea

Contributors

David Moores
Gérard Houllier
Ian Cotton
John Keith
Dave Ball
Ged Rea

Thanks to

The staff of Liverpool FC for their assistance in the production of this book including Rick Parry, Joe Corrigan, Steve Heighway, Hughie McAuley, Ian Cotton, Davide De Maestri and Kate Thompson

Photographs

Allsport, Action Images, Liverpool Post and Echo

Design and editorial

designsection Frome

First published in 2000 by

Granada Media, an imprint of
Andre Deutsch Limited
76 Dean Street, London W1V 5HA
for **Liverpool Football Club**
in association with **Granada Media**

ISBN
0 233 99886 1

Printed and bound in the UK by
Butler & Tanner Ltd, Frome and London

contents

LIVERPOOL
FOOTBALL CLUB

CHAIRMAN	**D.R. MOORES**
CHIEF EXECUTIVE	**R.N. PARRY BSC FCA**
DIRECTORS (with effect from 1 July 2000)	**N. WHITE FSCA** **T.D. SMITH** **K.E.B. CLAYTON FCA** **J. BURNS**
VICE-PRESIDENT	**H.E. ROBERTS**
TEAM MANAGER	**GERARD HOULLIER**
SECRETARY	**W.B. MORRISON**

CLUB HONOURS

LEAGUE CHAMPIONS	**1900-01**	**1905-06**	**1921-22**	**1922-23**	**1946-47**
	1963-64	**1965-66**	**1972-73**	**1975-76**	**1976-77**
	1978-79	**1979-80**	**1981-82**	**1982-83**	**1983-84**
	1985-86	**1987-88**	**1989-90**		
EUROPEAN CUP WINNERS	**1976-77**	**1977-78**	**1980-81**	**1983-84**	
EUROPEAN SUPER CUP WINNERS	**1977**				
U.E.F.A. CUP WINNERS	**1972-73**	**1975-76**			
FA CUP WINNERS	**1964-65**	**1973-74**	**1985-86**	**1988-89**	**1991-92**
LEAGUE CUP/MILK CUP WINNERS	**1980-81**	**1981-82**	**1982-83**	**1983-84**	
COCA-COLA CUP WINNERS	**1994-95**				

MESSAGE FROM THE CHAIRMAN

I am delighted in welcoming everybody to the club's new Official Year Book that the name of Liverpool FC will once again be included in European competition. It is where we want to be and qualifying for Europe was our prime aim at the start of last season both from a prestige and financial viewpoint.

It reflects great credit on Gérard Houllier and his playing squad, many of them playing in English football for the first time, that they were still competing for a Champions' League qualifying place right up to the last game of last season.

As events turned out we finished fourth to confirm our entry into the UEFA Cup, a competition in which we have enjoyed memorable success in the past. Europe has played a massive part in the history and tradition of our club and we look forward hopefully to more achievement in the Continental arena in the future.

I feel we have made tremendous progress when you take into account not only the fact that we had so many foreign players having to adjust to the English game but also our injury problems last season. We were severely hit in attack with Michael Owen and Robbie Fowler missing large chunks of the campaign and playing alongside each other only rarely.

I doubt if many clubs would be able to withstand the extended absence of two such world class players and still make it a season of achievement by finishing so high and qualifying for Europe. We were also robbed of our club captain Jamie Redknapp for long periods while Vladimir Smicer, one of last summer's arrivals, also had a season bedevilled by injury and illness. When fully fit he will be like a new signing for Gérard.

The past year has included a landmark event both for Liverpool FC and myself with the departure of Peter Robinson from Anfield after 35 years as secretary, chief executive and, latterly, executive vice chairman. As well as being a constant tower of strength and efficiency for the club through days of triumph and, sadly, tragedy Peter has been a wonderful friend and colleague to me. What he's done for Liverpool and for me is beyond estimation.

Apparently, Peter and Roy Jones – his former assistant who has also just cut his ties with the club after more than half a century of service – worked out that since Peter's arrival in 1965 Liverpool have played 999 home games watched by some 38 million spectators. In that period the club have won 27 major trophies.

It's an astounding record and personally, I feel sad about Peter leaving the club because he's been a friend of mine for 25 years. Needless to say, we wish him every success in whatever the future holds for him.

We are fortunate to have in our chief executive Rick Parry, a man we believe can take the club through the challenge of the 21st century. And, as far as I'm concerned, our home will remain Anfield. There has been a welter of media speculation that we may leave for a new ground but it is the club's adamant intention not only to stay at Anfield but, given planning permission, to turn it into a 60,000-seat stadium to rank with the finest anywhere.

I would like to conclude by wishing all our supporters at home and abroad a very successful and enjoyable year.

DAVID MOORES

My admiration for Liverpool Football Club spans many years and I have fond memories of attending European nights at Anfield as a spectator during my teaching days on Merseyside in the late 1960s and early 1970s.

That is why, overall, I am delighted at the sound progress and improvement the team has made in the past year and achieved a return to European competition in the UEFA Cup.

Naturally, there was disappointment that we just missed out on a Champions League qualifying place but the fact that we were competing for third place in the Premiership right up to the final match of last season underlines the progress we have made.

We finished three places higher and 13 points better than the previous season and we secured a UEFA Cup place with two matches still to play. So we are on the way to something and we are ahead of schedule.

In September last season not many people would have believed we would finish in the top four but the players responded with a run that matched that of champions Manchester United until the last few games.

And one factor that tends to be overlooked is that the average age of our team last season was 23.9 years, the youngest of any Premiership club. Manchester United's was 27.9 years so there is a four-year gap and our team needs time to mature and grow together.

But they qualified for Europe despite long absences through injury of Robbie Fowler, Michael Owen, Jamie Redknapp, Vladimir Smicer and Vegard Heggem. So our progress has been encouraging. I have to look at the overall picture because what I am engaged in at this club is a four-year strategy to re-establish Liverpool among the foremost clubs in the country.

I am looking for balance in the squad and I feel we have the right blend of foreign and English players, many of whom have been developed at this club, which I believe is very important.

Our squad will be strengthened by the arrival of Markus Babbel, and one or two other signings, and we will be looking to build on the progress already made.

If our players show the same workrate and attitude and display the strength, consistency and efficiency of performance they did for much of last season, then I firmly believe the new season will be one of further achievement. I can assure all our supporters that is the aim of us all.

GERARD HOULLIER

august

Saturday 7   v   SHEFFIELD WEDNESDAY   A
Saturday 14   v   WATFORD   H
Saturday 21   v   MIDDLESBROUGH   A
Monday 23   v   LEEDS UNITED   A
Saturday 28   v   ARSENAL   H

Sheffield Wednesday | 1

VENUE: Hillsborough, 3.00pm

ATTENDANCE: 34,853

REFEREE: Graham Poll (Tring)

SCORER: Carbone 88

28 **SRNICEK**

19 **NEWSOME**

6 **WALKER**

5 **THOME**

3 **HINCHCLIFFE**

18 **DONNELLY**

16 **ALEXANDERSSON**

7 **SONNER**

14 **RUDI**

23 **DE BILDE**

9 **SIBON**

substitutes

1 **PRESSMAN**

22 **HASLAM**

21 **BRISCOE**
(for 18) 78 mins

8 **CARBONE**
(for 23) 69 mins

12 **CRESSWELL**
(for 9) 59 mins

Robbie Fowler led the Reds' line superbly, but had to wait until late in the game for his goal.

> *'I was delighted with Robbie Fowler. After his earlier miss he might have thought, "It's not my day". But he kept working tremendously hard right to the end and scored a very important goal.'* – Gérard Houllier

Gérard Houllier's first full season as sole Liverpool manager began victoriously thanks to late goals from Robbie Fowler and Titi Camara. The latter was one of seven foreign summer signings and all but one made their senior Liverpool debuts at Hillsborough.

In the starting line-up were Dutch international goalkeeper Sander Westerveld (who cost £4 million from Vitesse Arnhem), Finland international centre back Sami Hyypia (£2.6 million from Dutch club Willem II), Czech Republic midfield star Vladimir Smicer (£4 million from French club Lens), German international midfielder Dietmar Hamann (£8 million from Newcastle) and Guinea striker Camara, who cost £2.7 million from Marseille.

2 Liverpool

SCORERS: Fowler 75
Camara 84

Another recruit, Dutch striker Erik Meijer, signed on a free transfer under the Bosman ruling from German club Bayer Leverkusen, just managed to make his Liverpool debut when he replaced Camara with a minute left on the clock.

Houllier's remaining summer capture, Swiss international centre back Stephane Henchoz who cost £3.5 million from Blackburn, was still recovering from groin surgery and ruled out along with hamstring casualty Michael Owen.

Liverpool had a scare when Wednesday's new Belgian signing Gilles de Bilde saw his 25-yard shot hit the bar early in a first half Liverpool generally controlled but which was marred by the departure of Hamann with ankle ligament damage that required surgery. The opening 45 minutes failed to produce a goal.

Early in the second half Robbie Fowler, appointed vice captain by Houllier, sent a close-range header over the bar after home goalkeeper Pavel Srnicek had parried a free kick from new Liverpool skipper Jamie Redknapp. But Fowler made amends by firing Liverpool ahead with a left foot strike from the impressive Smicer's precise pass.

Another Fowler blast ten minutes later was too hot for Srnicek to hold and Camara gleefully snapped up the rebound to claim his first senior Liverpool goal. Even though Benito Carbone's superb 'chip' reduced the margin Liverpool emerged with an encouraging win.

Titi Camara won the match with his first senior Liverpool goal.

WESTERVELD 1
HEGGEM 14
CARRAGHER 23
HYYPIA 12
MATTEO 21
SMICER 7
REDKNAPP 11
HAMANN 16
BERGER 15
CAMARA 22
FOWLER 9

substitutes
NIELSEN 26
SONG 4
THOMPSON 25
(for 16) 24 mins
STAUNTON 5
(for 25) 82 mins
MEIJER 18
(for 22) 90 mins

VENUE: **Anfield, 3.00pm**

ATTENDANCE: **44,174**

REFEREE: **Alan Wilkie (Chester-le-Street)**

1 **WESTERVELD**

14 **HEGGEM**

23 **CARRAGHER**

12 **HYYPIA**

21 **MATTEO**

28 **GERRARD**

11 **REDKNAPP**

15 **BERGER**

7 **SMICER**

22 **CAMARA**

9 **FOWLER**

substitutes

19 **FRIEDEL**

5 **STAUNTON**

4 **SONG**
(for 14) 81 mins

25 **THOMPSON**
(for 28) 57 mins

13 **RIEDLE**
(for 7) 72 mins

The agony of Liverpool and their supporters was encapsulated in the Sunday newspaper banner headline which proclaimed: 'Mooney talks as Reds are humbled.'

The Mooney referred to was Watford's Tommy whose decisive goal for the newly promoted visitors, who gained Premiership status via the First Division play-offs, stunned an expectant Anfield leaving Gérard Houllier admitting: 'I did not recognise my team.'

Liverpool fans had arrived to witness the first home game of Houllier's French revolution which, as well as ushering in a host of new arrivals, had also seen the

Jamie Radknapp brings the ball out of defence in seach of an equaliser.

departures of Steve McManaman, David James, Paul Ince, Oyvind Leonhardsen, Rob Jones, Sean Dundee, Jean Michel Ferri and Tony Warner.

But the artisans of hard working Watford inflicted a shock defeat on Houllier's reconstructed forces thanks to Liverpool's familiar, haunting lack of a killer instinct. They made chances but spurned them. And when Liverpool efforts were on target they were denied by Watford goalkeeper Chris Day.

Liverpool, for whom promising teenager Steven Gerrard replaced the injured Hamann, were given a warning of what was to come when Mooney's long range strike demanded a fine save from Sander Westerveld.

But in the 16th minute he was beaten after Peter Kennedy's right flank free kick deflected off Robbie Fowler's head, Vegard Heggem's attempted clearance hit Dominic Matteo and former Liverpool fan Mooney accepted the close range chance to complete a personal record of scoring in all four divisions.

Jamie Redknapp, Patrik Berger and Gerrard all had chances to level the score. But in the later stages, when Liverpool lost ankle ligament victim Vladimir Smicer, Watford almost doubled their lead, substitute Rigobert Song heading off the line from Micah Hyde.

1 Watford

SCORER: Mooney 15

> *'Little wonder that Watford boss Graham Taylor, a wine buff who presented Houllier with a 1998 vintage bottle of Chateau Lagrange before the game, was tempted to buy his jubilant players a whole crate of the precious stuff.'* – Peter Fitton, The Mail on Sunday

Mooney's goal, though, was enough to make it Lucky 13 for Watford... their first ever top flight reward on Merseyside after losing on their previous 12 visits.

DAY 13
LYTTLE 2
KENNEDY 3
PALMER 5
PAGE 4
ROBINSON 6
NGONGE 7
HYDE 8
MOONEY 9
JOHNSON 10
WILLIAMS 32

substitutes
GUDMUNDSSON 20
BONNOT 24
WALKER 34
FOLEY 33
(for 7) 69 mins
EASTON 19
(for 10) 58 mins

Dominic Matteo goes down under a strong challenge from Watford's Clint Easton.

Middlesbrough | 1

VENUE: The Riverside, 3.00pm
ATTENDANCE: 34,783
REFEREE: Steve Dunn (Bristol)

SCORER: Deane 49

1 **SCHWARZER**
14 **STAMP**
4 **VICKERS**
5 **FESTA**
6 **PALLISTER**
9 **INCE**
16 **TOWNSEND**
8 **GASCOIGNE**
17 **ZIEGE**
19 **RICARD**
10 **DEANE**

substitutes

25 **ROBERTS**
15 **MADDISON**
7 **MUSTOE**
(for 14) 84 mins
11 **O'NEILL**
(for 8) 19 mins
18 **CAMPBELL**
(for 19) 88 mins

Boro's new signing Christian Ziege challenges Vegard Heggem for midfield supremacy.

0   Liverpool

A second consecutive defeat for Liverpool left them languishing in 17th place in the Premiership – one place above the relegation zone – after the season's opening three games.

It was another example of Liverpool domination going unrewarded as they fell to the game's only goal, scored by Brian Deane four minutes into the second half.

The biting frustration for Liverpool was that in Boro's first real attack of the game Christian Ziege and Keith O'Neill combined for the German to move into the box and deliver a cross that Deane turned past Sander Westerveld.

Jamie Redknapp rises to clear from the influential Christian Ziege.

> **'Liverpool's most immediate concern lies with an attack that has managed only two goals in three games and, as Houllier so eloquently put it, "lacks scoring efficiency".**
>
> **'There should be a handy solution to that when Michael Owen completes his rehabilitation from a hamstring injury.'**
>
> *– Garry Doolan,* Liverpool Daily Post

The duel at the Riverside Stadium pitted Liverpool against their former captain Paul Ince, whose sale by Houllier less than a month earlier for £1.25 million clearly shocked the England midfielder and led to him unleashing a public blast in Anfield's direction.

But Ince kept his cool and even acted as peacemaker in a flare up after a challenge by the highly impressive Steven Gerrard on Boro's Phil Stamp.

Smicer's enforced absence meant a starting place for Steve Staunton in a three-at-the-back formation with Jamie Carragher and Sami Hyypia. Vegard Heggem and Dominic Matteo filled the wing back roles in a side also stripped of the injured Hamann, Henchoz and Owen while teenage French defender Djimi Traore was named in the 16 for the first time as a substitute.

Liverpool's hopes of an equaliser disappeared when Camara's shot from 20 yards swerved narrowly wide before the African striker had another powerful effort saved by Mark Schwarzer. At the other end Hamilton Ricard let Liverpool off the hook by firing over from a clear chance. This was a poor result for Liverpool whose urgent task was to start scoring goals.

WESTERVELD 1
HEGGEM 14
CARRAGHER 23
HYYPIA 12
MATTEO 21
STAUNTON 5
GERRARD 28
REDKNAPP 11
BERGER 15
CAMARA 22
FOWLER 9

substitutes
FRIEDEL 19
SONG 4
THOMPSON 25
(for 15) 65 mins
TRAORE 30
MEIJER 18
(for 5) 73 mins

Leeds United 1

VENUE: Elland Road, 8.00pm
ATTENDANCE: 39,703
REFEREE: David Elleray (Harrow-on-the-Hill)

SCORER: Song (o.g.) 20

1 **MARTYN**
18 **MILLS**
5 **RADEBE**
6 **WOODGATE**
3 **HARTE**
23 **BATTY**
11 **BOWYER**
10 **KEWELL**
7 **HOPKIN**
8 **BRIDGES**
12 **HUCKERBY**

substitutes

19 **BAKKE**
(for 7) 68 mins
2 **KELLY**
13 **ROBINSON**
22 **DUBERRY**
17 **SMITH**
(for 8) 56 mins

Patrik Berger, who was
involved in both of
Liverpool's goals.

Newly appointed Liverpool captain Jamie Redknapp gave an assured display at Elland Road as Gérard Houllier's team deservedly dispelled fears of the club making their worst start to a season for 75 years.

Not since the opening of the 1924-25 campaign had Liverpool lost three and won only one of their first four games. And Leeds found their opponents in no mood to etch an unwanted niche in the record books.

> *'Elland Road continues to be a happy hunting ground for Liverpool, who now boast a record of ten wins and only three defeats in 18 visits stretching back to Kevin Keegan's bubble-permed pomp.'*
> *– Phil Shaw, The* Independent

'Redknapp ran the game,' admitted Leeds boss David O'Leary, whose team was second best to a determined Liverpool who had Rigobert Song and David Thompson in the starting line up in place of a fifth injury absentee, Vegard Heggem, and Steve Staunton, who switched to the bench.

Houllier reverted to a 4-4-2 formation which was denied the lead through Lee Bowyer's dramatic diving headed clearance from Redknapp's blistering shot. They then suffered the blow of falling behind to a 20th-minute Song own goal when Ian Harte's corner sailed over the defence and spun into the net off the Cameroon full back.

Liverpool, though, shrugged off that jolting setback and Patrik Berger went close before the lively Titi Camara crowned a fine personal performance with a spectacular equaliser in first-half stoppage time. Camara and Berger linked and when the ball broke from Lucas Radebe's challenge on the Czech midfielder

2 Liverpool

SCORERS: **Camara 45**

Radebe (o.g.) 55

Steven Gerrard congratulates Titi Camara on his spectacular equaliser just before the break.

WESTERVELD 1
SONG 4
CARRAGHER 23
HYYPIA 12
MATTEO 21
THOMPSON 25
GERRARD 28
REDKNAPP 11
BERGER 15
CAMARA 22
FOWLER 9

substitutes
FRIEDEL 19
STAUNTON 5
MURPHY 24
TRAORE 30
MEIJER 18

Camara dispatched a shot from just outside the box which went over Nigel Martyn and off the underside of the bar into the top corner of the net.

Ten minutes after the interval Berger was again involved in the move which secured Liverpool's victory, courtesy of the game's second own goal. Robbie Fowler and Radebe battled to reach Berger's cross from the left... and it ended with the South African defender diverting the ball past his own goalkeeper Martyn.

But it was a worthy win that hoisted Liverpool to ninth in the Premiership and after a victory hug for his assistant Phil Thompson, Houllier declared: 'The best compliment you can have when you come off the field is for the opposition manager to say you deserved it.' With Redknapp in such fine form the outlook for Liverpool was suddenly more optimistic.

Liverpool 2

VENUE: Anfield, 3.00pm

ATTENDANCE: 44,886

REFEREE: Dermot Gallagher (Banbury)

SCORERS: Fowler 8

Berger 76

1 **WESTERVELD**

4 **SONG**

23 **CARRAGHER**

12 **HYYPIA**

21 **MATTEO**

28 **GERRARD**

11 **REDKNAPP**

15 **BERGER**

25 **THOMPSON**

22 **CAMARA**

9 **FOWLER**

substitutes

19 **FRIEDEL**

5 **STAUNTON**

14 **HEGGEM**
(for 25) 70 mins

10 **OWEN**
(for 22) 87 mins

18 **MEIJER**

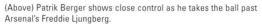

(Above) Patrik Berger shows close control as he takes the ball past Arsenal's Freddie Ljungberg.

(Right) Robbie Fowler and Martin Keown perform an aerial ballet.

The much vaunted Gunners were shot down by a brilliant Liverpool display on a day that brought many personal celebrations amidst a superbly cohesive performance from an unchanged team. There was heady anticipation sparked by Gérard Houllier's choice of Michael Owen on the substitute bench, his first inclusion in the 16 since damaging his hamstring against Leeds the previous April.

In the event it was his strike colleague Robbie Fowler who brought Anfield to its feet by breaking the deadlock with just eight minutes 13 seconds on the clock. The England forward's tenth goal in 12 outings against Arsenal put the seal on a week in which he became a father, with the arrival of a 7lb 3oz daughter, Louise, and was also called up by his country. Dominic Matteo, making his 100th League appearance for Liverpool, was involved in the build-up with Steven Gerrard and Patrik Berger before Fowler, some 25 yards out, connected with his left foot and left absent David

0 Arsenal

Seaman's deputy Alex Manninger helpless as the ball flew in off the underside of the bar.

Arsenal escaped further punishment when Manninger palmed over a Fowler shot, Berger's shot grazed a post and another Fowler effort struck an upright. But they were breached again 14 minutes from time. A free kick awarded for a foul on Jamie Redknapp gave Berger the chance to unleash his left foot and his shot deflected off Fredrik Ljungberg and beat the stranded Manninger.

The ecstatic Kop fans had more delight to come, first when Owen made his reappearance as substitute for Titi Camara with three minutes left on the clock and, second, when goalkeeper Sander Westerveld saved Davor Suker's stoppage-time penalty, awarded after Rigobert Song was judged to have fouled Ljungberg.

'In a few days we have beaten two title contenders in Leeds and Arsenal. We never managed to beat any of the top four last season. A cracker by Robbie unlocked the game. He was something special today and we have to congratulate all the players.' – Gérard Houllier

MANNINGER 13
DIXON 2
WINTERBURN 3
KEOWN 5
ADAMS 6
VIEIRA 4
HENRY 14
LJUNGBERG 8
OVERMARS 11
PARLOUR 15
BERGKAMP 10

substitutes
SUKER 9
(for 11) 64 mins
SILVINHO 16
(for 15) 75 mins
VIVAS 7
UPSON 20
LUKIC 24

Jamie Redknapp, Robbie Fowler and Steven Gerrard acclaim Patrik Berger's 76th-minute strike.

Saturday 7	v	SHEFFIELD WEDNESDAY	A	2-1
Saturday 14	v	WATFORD	H	0-1
Saturday 21	v	MIDDLESBROUGH	A	0-1
Monday 23	v	LEEDS UNITED	A	2-1
Saturday 28	v	ARSENAL	H	2-0

9

ROBBIE FOWLER

PLAYER OF THE MONTH

A superb scoring performance by Fowler against Arsenal, watched by admiring England manager Kevin Keegan, applied a positive finish to a curtain-raising month of fluctuating fortunes for Liverpool. But the shock of losing their opening home game to newly promoted Watford and the frustration of an unlucky defeat at Middlesbrough were dispelled by morale-boosting conquests of Leeds and Arsenal.

	P	W	D	L	F	A	Pts
Manchester United	5	4	1	0	11	3	13
Aston Villa	5	3	1	1	7	3	10
Arsenal	5	3	1	1	7	4	10
Tottenham Hotspur	4	3	0	1	8	5	9
Middlesbrough	5	3	0	2	7	7	9
Chelsea	3	2	1	0	7	2	7
Everton	5	2	1	2	11	8	7
Leicester City	5	2	1	2	8	6	7
West Ham United	3	2	1	0	5	3	7
Leeds United	5	2	1	2	6	5	7
Sunderland	5	2	1	2	5	7	7
LIVERPOOL	4	2	0	2	4	4	6
Watford	5	2	0	3	4	6	6
Southampton	4	2	0	2	6	9	6
Wimbledon	5	1	2	2	9	13	5
Coventry City	5	1	1	3	4	5	4
Bradford City	4	1	1	2	2	4	4
Derby County	5	1	1	3	4	7	4
Newcastle United	5	0	1	4	7	13	1
Sheffield Wednesday	5	0	1	4	3	11	1

UP TO AND INCLUDING WEDNESDAY 25 AUGUST 1999

'Talking Points'

- 7/8/99 Liverpool's opening day success at Hillsborough means **they have lost only once** in their first game in the last 18 years. That was in August 1992 at Nottingham Forest.

- 28/8/99 **Liverpool have won five and drawn two** of the last seven games **played at Anfield** against Arsenal. In those games only Ian Wright with a penalty in 1995-96 has scored for the Gunners.

- 28/8/99 **Sander Westerveld** kept his first **clean sheet** for the club in a game which was Arsene Wenger's 150th in charge of Arsenal.

'Talking Points'

for more info visit www.liverpoolfc.net

september

Saturday 11	v	MANCHESTER UNITED	H
Tuesday 14	v	HULL CITY	A
Saturday 18	v	LEICESTER CITY	A
Tuesday 21	v	HULL CITY	H
Monday 27	v	EVERTON	H

Liverpool 2

VENUE: Anfield, 11.30am
ATTENDANCE: 44,929
REFEREE: Graham Barber (Tring)

SCORERS: Hyypia 23
Berger 68

'The games between us have got more exciting in recent years. Our first half show was superb but we had to ride our luck in the second half when Liverpool proved their worth.' – Sir Alex Ferguson

1 WESTERVELD
4 SONG
23 CARRAGHER
12 HYYPIA
21 MATTEO
28 GERRARD
11 REDKNAPP
15 BERGER
25 THOMPSON
22 CAMARA
9 FOWLER

substitutes

19 FRIEDEL
5 STAUNTON
14 HEGGEM
(for 28) 64 mins
10 OWEN
(for 22) 64 mins
7 SMICER
(for 25) 46 mins

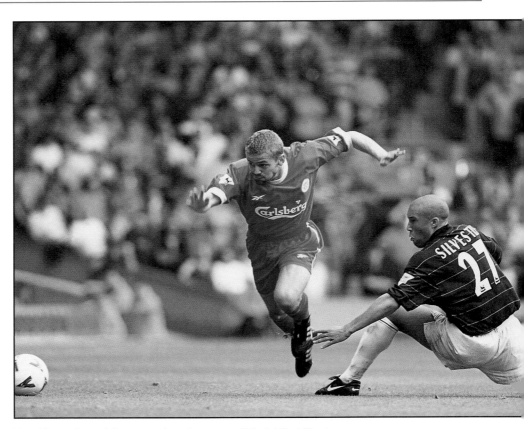

Vegard Heggem is a study in concentration as he races past United's Mikael Silvestre.

Three first half goals by the Treble-winning visitors proved too much of a mountain for Liverpool to climb and the 11.30 kick off signalled an agonising morning for Jamie Carragher. The Liverpool defender conceded two own goals, the first of them after only four minutes when he headed a Ryan Giggs near-post cross past Sander Westerveld as he attempted to clear.

3 Manchester United

SCORERS: **Carragher 3, 44 (2 o.gs.)**
Cole 18

United doubled their lead when David Beckham, ever threatening on the right flank, took a free kick and Andy Cole was allowed a free header to collect his eighth League goal against Liverpool.

But Sami Hyypia reignited Liverpool hopes with his first goal for the club, headed in after United's debutant Italian goalkeeper Massimo Taibi, a £4.5 million signing from Venezia, misjudged the flight of a Jamie Redknapp free kick.

Both sides had penalty claims rejected by Graham Barber, who was the first referee to be in radio contact with his assistants on the lines. He was unmoved, though, when Nicky Butt appeared to handle in a tussle with Rigobert Song and when Giggs seemed to be pulled back by the shirt by David Thompson.

United struck again just before the break and it was another Beckham right-flank cross that did the damage. Henning Berg connected and his header rebounded onto Song and off the hapless Carragher into the net.

Gérard Houllier re-shuffled his forces after the interval when Vladimir Smicer replaced David Thompson in a 3-5-2 formation that seized the initiative. Further changes came a few minutes later when Owen and Heggem replaced Camara and Gerrard. However, they could

Robbie Fowler gets his head down to go past Jaap Stam.

not seize any points reward even though Patrik Berger accepted Dominic Matteo's pass and reduced the arrears after 68 minutes.

Taibi atoned for his earlier lapse with superb saves from Smicer and Robbie Fowler as United, who had Cole sent off for aiming a kick at Song, held out for their seventh win in a run of nine unbeaten games against Liverpool.

TAIBI 26
NEVILLE P 12
STAM 6
BERG 21
SILVESTRE 27
GIGGS 11
BUTT 8
SCHOLES 18
BECKHAM 7
COLE 9
YORKE 19

substitutes
SHERINGHAM 10
VAN DER GOUW 17
SOLSKJAER 20
WALLWORK 30
(for 8) 39 mins
CLEGG 23
(for 12) 83 mins

Hull City 1

VENUE: Boothferry Park, 7.45pm
ATTENDANCE: 10,034
REFEREE: Ken Leach (Codsall)

SCORER: Brown 58

1 **BRACEY**
3 **HARPER**
2 **MANN**
8 **GREAVES**
7 **EDWARDS**
5 **WHITTLE**
22 **BRABIN**
19 **SCHOFIELD**
11 **D'AURIA**
9 **BROWN**
10 **EYRE**

substitutes

17 **SWALES**
(for 2) 31 mins
20 **ALCIDE**
(for 11) 56 mins
18 **WOOD**
(for 10) 73 mins
15 **WILLIAMS**
25 **BAKER**

Liverpool's break from Premiership action for Worthington Cup duty gave French defender Djimi Traore, a £550,000 signing from Laval the previous February, his debut outing at centre back alongside Sami Hyypia. The game also saw Michael Owen make his first senior start of the season, following two comeback outings as a substitute, while Danny Murphy and Dutch striker Erik Meijer crowned their first starts of the campaign with a brace of goals apiece… their first goals for Liverpool.

Murphy opened the scoring when he met a low tenth-minute cross from Vladimir Smicer, who was withdrawn at half time with hamstring damage and replaced by his fellow Czech, Patrik Berger. Just after Liverpool's Third Division opponents had seen Gary Brabin's shot beat Sander Westerveld but rebound off a post Murphy plundered a second goal after Meijer had controlled David Thompson's right wing cross.

Meijer made it 3-0 soon after the interval. Thompson was again the provider from the right and the big striker fired low into the far corner from just inside the box.

Erik Meijer had a fantastic game, scoring two second-half goals.

5 Liverpool

SCORERS: **Murphy 10, 30**
Meijer 48, 75
Staunton 89

Danny Murphy accepts the congratulations of his team-mates after opening the scoring.

WESTERVELD 1
STAUNTON 5
CARRAGHER 23
HYYPIA 12
HEGGEM 14
TRAORE 30
THOMPSON 25
MURPHY 24
SMICER 7
MEIJER 18
OWEN 10

substitutes
FRIEDEL 19
SONG 4
BJORNEBYE 20
BERGER 15
(for 7) 46 mins
CAMARA 22
(for 10) 76 mins

'The good thing was the way we took the game extremely professionally. The commitment was there. We responded well to Hull's physical pressure and once we got the ball on the ground we passed it around and did well.' – Gérard Houllier

Slackness in defence by Liverpool allowed Hull the freedom to reduce the deficit when a John Eyre corner was flicked on by John Schofield for David Brown to score. But another goal from Meijer, who lofted the ball over the keeper following a long run by Vegard Heggem, and a Steve Staunton strike a minute from the end ensured a scoreline that reflected Liverpool's superiority and rendered the second leg a formality.

Leicester City 2

VENUE: Filbert Street, 3.00pm

ATTENDANCE: 21,623

REFEREE: Uriah Rennie (Sheffield)

SCORERS: Cottee 2

Izzet 86

22 **ARPHEXAD**

3 **SINCLAIR**

18 **ELLIOTT**

4 **TAGGART**

11 **GUPPY**

6 **IZZET**

14 **SAVAGE**

7 **LENNON**

24 **IMPEY**

27 **COTTEE**

9 **HESKEY**

substitutes

29 **OAKES**
(for 24) 60 mins

15 **GILCHRIST**
(for 27) 66 mins

21 **FENTON**

34 **FETTIS**

37 **ZAGORAKIS**

Michael Owen appears to be held back as he tries to go past Robbie Savage.

There were just 81 seconds on the clock when Tony Cottee, a familiar Liverpool adversary from his Everton days, put Leicester ahead. A mistake by Dominic Matteo let in Muzzy Izzet who sent Cottee clean through to score.

Liverpool went into the game without ankle casualty Robbie Fowler but Michael Owen celebrated his first Premiership start since April with an impressive two-goal performance, watched by England boss Kevin Keegan.

Owen's pleasure, however, was not without pain. He was flattened by Matt Elliott's elbow in a second half tussle with the Leicester captain seen by millions on BBC TV's *Match of the Day*. Although Elliott was not penalised by referee Uriah Rennie the Leicester man apologised and insisted there was no malicious intent.

Owen had put Liverpool level from the penalty spot after Patrik Berger had been fouled in a sandwich between Gerry Taggart and Elliott. A great run by Titi Camara from deep in his own half to the edge of the Leicester box heralded Liverpool's second goal shortly before the break.

2 Liverpool

SCORERS: Owen 23 (penalty), 39

> *'It was great to be back in the side and to score twice. But it wasn't important that I scored. I was more interested in the team result. I'd have settled for me not scoring and the team winning 1-0. We've got to improve on that performance.'* – Michael Owen

Camara found Matteo who atoned for his early blunder with a pass for Owen to side-foot his side in front. Soon after the interval Leicester were reduced to ten men when Frank Sinclair was dismissed for a second booking after a late challenge on Camara, which led to the injured Guinea striker being replaced by Erik Meijer.

Liverpool, with Owen in sprightly form, should have clinched victory but paid the price for spurning chances when Izzet snatched a Leicester equaliser by latching onto Elliott's pass and firing past Sander Westerveld. The agony was complete for Gérard Houllier and his side when David Thompson was sent off in the last minute for a second yellow card after fouling Robbie Savage.

WESTERVELD 1
MATTEO 21
CARRAGHER 23
HYYPIA 12
HEGGEM 14
GERRARD 28
THOMPSON 25
REDKNAPP 11
BERGER 15
CAMARA 22
OWEN 10

substitutes
FRIEDEL 19
SONG 4
STAUNTON 5
MURPHY 24
(for 11) 78 mins
MEIJER 18
(for 22) 55 mins

Erik Meijer shrugs off the challenge of Stefan Oakes.

Liverpool 4

VENUE: Anfield, 7.45pm
ATTENDANCE: 24,318
REFEREE: John Brandwood (Lichfield)

SCORERS: Murphy 33
Maxwell 46
Riedle 65, 89

Liverpool win 9-3 on aggregate

19 **FRIEDEL**
4 **SONG**
30 **TRAORE**
2 **HENCHOZ**
5 **STAUNTON**
7 **SMICER**
25 **THOMPSON**
24 **MURPHY**
33 **MAXWELL**
18 **MEIJER**
13 **RIEDLE**

substitutes

31 **KIPPE**
(for 7) 67 mins
32 **NEWBY**
(for 2) 75 mins
14 **HEGGEM**
(for 24) 46 mins
26 **NIELSEN**
28 **GERRARD**

Gérard Houllier made ten changes from the team that had played at Leicester including debuts for Swiss defender Stephane Henchoz, midfielder Layton Maxwell and substitutes Frode Kippe, a Norwegian defender signed from Lillestroem, and locally-born striker Jon Newby. In addition Djimi Traore and Erik Meijer made their home debuts against lowly visitors who trailed 5-1 from the first leg and then conceded another goal when Danny Murphy headed in Steve Staunton's 33rd minute cross.

Hull then suffered the misfortune of having their goalkeeper Lee Bracey sent off for handling outside his area, which meant substitute keeper Matthew Baker going on and Jamie Wood being withdrawn.

St Asaph-born Maxwell raised the curtain on the second half in spectacular style. The 19-year-old Wales Under 21 international, a product of Liverpool's Academy, cut in from the left,

Danny Murphy heads Liverpool's opening goal after 33 minutes.

2 | Hull City

SCORERS: Eyre 51 (penalty)
Alcide 56

evaded a challenge and dispatched a right foot shot into the Kop net to ensure it was a debut he would not forget.

Soon after that memorable strike Hull pulled a goal back when John Eyre coolly beat Brad Friedel from a penalty after David Thompson had handled the ball in the area. They soon added another through Colin Alcide's chip over Friedel to put them level on the night.

But battle-honed Karl Heinz Riedle spared Liverpool blushes against their ten-man foes with a brace of goals, the first from a low shot and the second with a header from Newby's cross. It proved a stylish Anfield goodbye for the German striker who joined Fulham for £200,000 a week later.

> *'I can't really explain my feelings when my shot went in. It is like a dream to be honest. I still can't believe it now. I just remember closing my eyes and running away. I wish I'd run towards the Kop now! My mum, dad, uncle and little sister were at the game, which was brilliant for me. I'm 20 in a few weeks so my goal was an early birthday present.'* – scoring debutant Layton Maxwell

BRACEY 1
HARPER 3
WILLIAMS 15
EDWARDS 7
WHITTLE 5
BRABIN 22
SCHOFIELD 19
WOOD 18
BROWN 9
EYRE 10
ALCIDE 20

substitutes
SWALES 17
D'AURIA 11
(for 19) 78 mins
BAKER 25
(for 18) 36 mins
HARRIS 16
(for 20) 67 mins
MORGAN 23

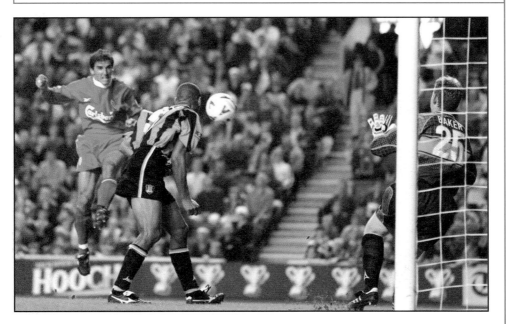

Karl Heinz Riedle heads Liverpool's fourth goal seconds before the final whistle.

Liverpool | 0

VENUE: Anfield, 8.00pm
ATTENDANCE: 44,802
REFEREE: Mike Riley (Rotherham)

1 **WESTERVELD**
14 **HEGGEM**
12 **HYYPIA**
23 **CARRAGHER**
5 **STAUNTON**
7 **SMICER**
16 **HAMANN**
11 **REDKNAPP**
15 **BERGER**
9 **FOWLER**
10 **OWEN**

substitutes

26 **NIELSEN**
2 **HENCHOZ**
22 **CAMARA**
(for 7) 70 mins
28 **GERRARD**
(for 16) 64 mins
18 **MEIJER**
(for 9) 64 mins

German midfielder Dietmar Hamann, injured on the season's opening day at Sheffield Wednesday, was plunged into his home debut against Liverpool's arch rivals on a night to forget for the Anfield club. Ankle casualty Robbie Fowler also returned but both he and Hamann were withdrawn midway through the second half of Merseyside's 161st League derby which was decided by Kevin Campbell's fourth minute finish from a Francis Jeffers pass.

Liverpool were rocked by the early goal and found it difficult to get into their usual fluent passing rhythm. It needed a save by Sander Westerveld from a Jeffers header to deny the young Everton striker a goal before Fowler had two shots saved by Paul Gerrard, who also kept out a 20-yard Jamie Redknapp effort.

It was a scrappy match with a number of niggly fouls and angry confrontations. A flurry of bookings by referee Mike Riley preceded a 77th minute clash between Westerveld and Jeffers who swapped punches and earned a red card apiece. As Liverpool had already used their three substitutes – Erik Meijer, Steven Gerrard and Titi Camara – it meant Steve Staunton taking over as stand-in keeper for the dismissed Dutchman.

The Irish defender proceeded to make a superb save to deny Abel Xavier while at the other end Paul Gerrard produced heroics for the visitors by somehow keeping out Meijer's shot, which deflected off Michael Ball, and then a Redknapp free kick.

But the evening was not so memorable for the Everton keeper's namesake. Liverpool's ranks were stripped to nine in the game's dying moments when substitute Steven Gerrard was shown the red card for a high challenge on Campbell.

Liverpool's defeat – their third in their last four home League games – meant that they trailed Everton by six points, had won only one of the last 11 Merseyside derbies and had not won a weekday duel with their neighbours since Bob Paisley's European champions triumphed 1-0 at Goodison through a David Johnson goal back in April 1978.

> *'Some of our players lost the plot. That's something I'm not used to and not happy about. Players have to keep their control and keep their nerve. How can you expect to control a game if you can't control yourself? What happened was unforgivable at this level and players must learn from it.' – Gérard Houllier*

1   Everton

SCORER: Campbell 4

GERRARD 13

DUNNE 15

WEIR 14

GOUGH 4

BALL 3

XAVIER 19

HUTCHISON 10

COLLINS 7

BARMBY 8

JEFFERS 17

CAMPBELL 9

substitutes

CLELAND 2

GEMMILL 11

WARD 21

JOHNSON 26

SIMONSEN 35

Michael Owen's face says it all on a stormy and disappointing evening for the Reds.

Saturday 11	v	MANCHESTER UNITED	H	2-3
Tuesday 14	v	HULL CITY	A	5-1
Saturday 18	v	LEICESTER CITY	A	2-2
Tuesday 21	v	HULL CITY	H	4-2
Monday 27	v	EVERTON	H	0-1

10

MICHAEL OWEN

PLAYER OF THE MONTH

The consolation for Liverpool in a disappointing month was the return of Michael Owen to senior action, illuminated by his two goals at Leicester. But anxieties over Robbie Fowler's fitness meant that the highly prized England pair started only one game together in September. Fate was to decree that this unfortunate trend would continue.

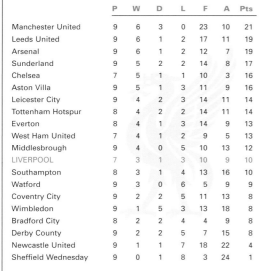

	P	W	D	L	F	A	Pts
Manchester United	9	6	3	0	23	10	21
Leeds United	9	6	1	2	17	11	19
Arsenal	9	6	1	2	12	7	19
Sunderland	9	5	2	2	14	8	17
Chelsea	7	5	1	1	10	3	16
Aston Villa	9	5	1	3	11	9	16
Leicester City	9	4	2	3	14	11	14
Tottenham Hotspur	8	4	2	2	14	11	14
Everton	8	4	1	3	14	9	13
West Ham United	7	4	1	2	9	5	13
Middlesbrough	9	4	0	5	10	13	12
LIVERPOOL	7	3	1	3	10	9	10
Southampton	8	3	1	4	13	16	10
Watford	9	3	0	6	5	9	9
Coventry City	9	2	2	5	11	13	8
Wimbledon	9	1	5	3	13	18	8
Bradford City	8	2	2	4	4	9	8
Derby County	9	2	2	5	7	15	8
Newcastle United	9	1	1	7	18	22	4
Sheffield Wednesday	9	0	1	8	3	24	1

UP TO AND INCLUDING SUNDAY 26 SEPTEMBER 1999

'Talking Points'

- 11/9/99 **Sami Hyypia**'s goal against Manchester United was his first for Liverpool. Liverpool's last win against United was in December 1995.

- 14/9/99 **Sander Westerveld** is only the **ninth man in the club's history** to keep goal in the League Cup.

- 21/9/99 In the return Littlewoods Cup game against Hull City – **Layton Maxwell scored on his debut.** The match also heralded the debuts of **Frode Kippe**, **Jon Newby** and **Stephane Henchoz.**

- 27/9/99 **Everton**'s win at **Anfield** was only their second in their last 14 visits.

'Talking Points'

for more info visit www.liverpoolfc.net

october

Saturday 2	v	ASTON VILLA	A
Wednesday 13	v	SOUTHAMPTON	A
Saturday 16	v	CHELSEA	H
Saturday 23	v	SOUTHAMPTON	A
Wednesday 27	v	WEST HAM UNITED	H

Aston Villa 0

VENUE: **Villa Park, 3.00pm**
ATTENDANCE: **39,217**
REFEREE: **Rob Harris (Oxford)**

39 **ENCKELMAN**
15 **BARRY**
4 **SOUTHGATE**
5 **EHIOGU**
24 **DELANEY**
17 **HENDRIE**
6 **BOATENG**
7 **TAYLOR**
11 **THOMPSON**
12 **JOACHIM**
9 **DUBLIN**

substitutes

13 **OAKES**
2 **WATSON**
34 **CALDERWOOD**
26 **STONE**
(for 17) 79 mins
10 **MERSON**
(for 6) 66 mins

A barren stalemate was memorable for the wrong reasons. Referee Rob Harris flourished his yellow card 11 times during the match and on the half hour sent off a stunned Steve Staunton, after showing him a second yellow and then red for alleged encroaching at a free kick.

But after studying video evidence the Oxford offical later rescinded Staunton's second yellow. The match result, however, was disappointing for Liverpool, who had gone into the game knowing that for a while they would be without the talents of Robbie Fowler because of the striker's ankle surgery the same day.

It meant that Erik Meijer came in for his first Premiership start, as did Stephane Henchoz in defence in which Rigobert Song was recalled at right back for Vegard Heggem.

Sami Hyypia makes sure there's no way past for Villa's Julian Joachim.

0 | Liverpool

Rigobert Song drives forward in a bid to break the deadlock.

WESTERVELD 1
SONG 4
STAUNTON 5
HYYPIA 12
HENCHOZ 2
SMICER 7
HAMANN 16
REDKNAPP 11
BERGER 15
MEIJER 18
OWEN 10

substitutes
NIELSEN 26
HEGGEM 14
GERRARD 28
(for 7) 30 mins
CARRAGHER 23
(for 16) 75 mins
CAMARA 22
(for 10) 80 mins

Despite being down to ten men for two thirds of the game the Liverpool rearguard – buttressed by Steven Gerarrd who replaced Vladimir Smicer in a re-shuffle after Staunton's exit – held firm. Behind them, goalkeeper Sander Westerveld dealt with everything Villa threw at him, including an early save from Julian Joachim after he had seized on an under-hit Henchoz back pass and a long range free kick from Alan Thompson.

When Villa did put the ball in the Liverpool net, through Dion Dublin's tap-in after Ugo Ehiogu had headed on Thompson's free kick, it was ruled out for offside. However, while Liverpool looked secure at the back their attacking contribution was below par, with their scoring attempts on a tight ration. Smicer went close with an angled shot that just beat the upright , Michael Owen deflected a Jamie Redknapp free kick wide and another free kick from the England midfielder and Liverpool captain demanded a good save low to his left from Peter Enckelman. But the goalless draw meant that Liverpool had gone four Premiership games without a win.

However, on the bright side Liverpool emerged with a clean sheet despite their defensive disruption caused by Staunton's dismissal.

> *'After being reduced to ten men for an hour of the game it was a*
> *wonderful exhibition of character by Liverpool, with Henchoz, Hyypia,*
> *Song and Gerrard magnificent in defence.'*
> – *Chris Bascombe,* Liverpool Echo

Southampton | 2

VENUE: **The Dell, 7.45pm**
ATTENDANCE: **13,822**
REFEREE: **Dermot Gallagher (Banbury)**

SCORERS: **Richards 67**
Soltvedt 90

1 **JONES**
2 **DODD**
6 **RICHARDS**
5 **LUNDEKVAM**
15 **BENALI**
30 **KACHLOUL**
32 **SOLTVEDT**
8 **OAKLEY**
14 **RIPLEY**
17 **PAHARS**
7 **LE TISSIER**

substitutes

4 **MARSDEN**
(for 8) 61 mins
16 **BEATTIE**
(for 14) 81 mins
10 **DAVIES**
(for 17) 75 mins
24 **COLLETER**
13 **MOSS**

An injury time strike from Trond Soltvedt sent Liverpool spinning out of the Worthington Cup to close a potential route into Europe and leave them reflecting on the cost of missed opportunities.

Michael Owen, scorer of their goal, could have had a hat trick but untypically spurned a batch of chances he would normally have taken in clinical style.

Goalkeeper Brad Friedel, taking over from suspended Sander Westerveld as Liverpool's last line of defence, was happy to see Matthew Oakley's long range volley whistle just over his bar before Owen had a chance to break the deadlock. But the England striker sidefooted wide after being put clean through by David Thompson, who was recalled after suspension to a team stripped of ankle casualties Robbie Fowler and Dietmar Hamann, banned Steven Gerrard and Vladimir Smicer, as a non-EEC national, as well as Westerveld.

When Thompson was again the provider, latching onto a poor back pass by Dean Richards early in the second half, Owen took full advantage with a right foot shot past Paul Jones to put Liverpool ahead, his 50th goal in 93 Liverpool outings.

Their lead, though, lasted only 14 minutes before the enigmatic Matt Le Tissier was involved in a Southampton equaliser. A challenge by Henchoz on Marian Pahars conceded a free kick which

Le Tissier duly delivered. Confusion reigned at the back for Liverpool and with Friedel stranded Dean Richards planted a header into an unguarded net.

Five minutes from the end Owen had the opportunity to see Liverpool into round four when Erik Meijer took a Jamie Redknapp pass, beat Claus Lundekvam and supplied his attacking colleague with an invitingly clear chance. But when Owen threw himself to the turf in frustrating self-recrimination, after shooting wide, it told its own story.

The sucker punch was applied in the final seconds when substitute Kevin Davies was given

Patrik Berger tries to find a way through the Saints' defence.

1 | Liverpool

SCORER: Owen 53

time to chip the ball over a static Liverpool defence to Soltvedt for the Norwegian to slide Southampton's winner past Friedel.

> *'You have to be indulgent with Michael, you have to be patient. It was only his fifth game back and sometimes you need more matches to get your season going. Nine times of ten he would have scored those goals but that is part of football life. I don't think it will bother him. We've had a chat and he will forget about it.'* – Gérard Houllier

FRIEDEL 19
STAUNTON 5
HENCHOZ 2
HYYPIA 12
SONG 4
CARRAGHER 23
THOMPSON 25
REDKNAPP 11
BERGER 15
MEIJER 18
OWEN 10

substitutes
NIELSEN 26
HEGGEM 14
(for 4) 74 mins
MATTEO 21
MURPHY 24
CAMARA 22
(for 25) 81 mins

Southampton's Stuart Ripley can only admire as Jamie Redknapp unleashes a shot on goal.

Liverpool 1

VENUE: Anfield, 3.00pm

ATTENDANCE: 44,826

REFEREE: Mike Reed (Birmingham)

SCORER: Thompson 48

19 **FRIEDEL**

4 **SONG**

12 **HYYPIA**

5 **STAUNTON**

2 **HENCHOZ**

7 **SMICER**

25 **THOMPSON**

11 **REDKNAPP**

23 **CARRAGHER**

24 **MURPHY**

10 **OWEN**

substitutes

26 **NIELSEN**

14 **HEGGEM**
(for 24) 80 mins

21 **MATTEO**

22 **CAMARA**

18 **MEIJER**
(for 10) 86 mins

A re-shaped Anfield side collected a prestigious victory in an eventful contest which saw Chelsea's artistry emerge second best to Liverpool's resolve despite Michael Owen's penalty miss. Chelsea arrived on Merseyside in fourth place on the back of a 5-0 thrashing of Manchester United in their previous Premiership outing and strengthened by the return of Marcel Desailly to the heart of their defence.

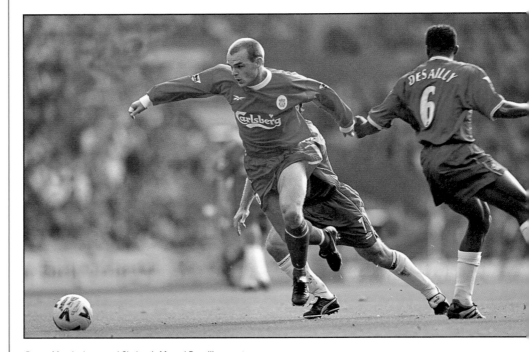

Danny Murphy 'nutmegs' Chelsea's Marcel Desailly.

The ultra cosmopolitan London club were pitted against a 12th placed Liverpool side which had Danny Murphy coming in for Erik Meijer in an advanced role behind Owen and with Vladimir Smicer replacing his fellow Czech, Patrik Berger.

The flowing action saw Murphy and Dennis Wise fire over at opposite ends and Jamie Redknapp's free kick beat Ed De Goey but just miss the target. And when the imperious Desailly found himself 'nutmegged' by Murphy it needed his French colleague Frank Leboeuf to rescue the situation before the former Crewe player could shoot.

Late in the first half Leboeuf switched his attentions to attack with a lofted pass into the

0 **Chelsea**

David Thompson stabs the ball past Ed de Goey to claim the points and the prestige from Chelsea.

> *'Chelsea have a truly dire record at Anfield, where they have won just one League game in 63 years. Liverpool, after a dispiriting run, were much relieved by this win. Their manager Gérard Houllier sought to inconvenience the defence with the best record in the Premiership by playing only one striker. The end justified the means.'*
> – *Joe Lovejoy,* The Sunday Times

DE GOEY 1
FERRER 17
DESAILLY 6
LEBOEUF 5
BABAYARO 3
PETRESCU 2
DESCHAMPS 7
WISE 11
POYET 8
ZOLA 25
SUTTON 9

substitutes

CUDICINI 23
MORRIS 20
LE SAUX 14
(for 5) 64 mins
LAMBOURDE 21
(for 2) 74 mins
FLO 19
(for 25) 68 mins

Liverpool box which found Gianfranco Zola. But the little Italian let Liverpool off the hook by volleying the chance straight at Brad Friedel.

Soon after the interval Liverpool prised a breakthrough that would give them victory. Steve Staunton's right-flank free kick was met by Rigobert Song's head and when Gustavo Poyet failed to clear David Thompson stabbed home his first goal of the season. It was only the fourth goal Chelsea had conceded in the Premiership and their fortunes went from bad to worse. They suffered the blow of losing the influential Leboeuf, who limped off injured after a challenge by Owen, which saw Graeme Le Saux sent on.

And then they had Leboeuf's centre back partner Desailly sent off after felling Murphy in the box and earning a second yellow card. But Owen sent his penalty wide of De Goey's right-hand post to keep Chelsea hopes alive.

Their substitute Tore Andre Flo fluffed a late Wise-created equalising chance by firing straight at Friedel and Chelsea's agony was complete when they were reduced to nine men through Wise's dismissal for retaliation on Smicer. It was Liverpool 's first 1-0 win in 72 games but hugely welcome and well deserved.

Southampton 1

VENUE: The Dell, 3.00pm

ATTENDANCE: 15,241

REFEREE: Neale Barry (Scunthorpe)

SCORER: Soltvedt 39

1 **JONES**

2 **DODD**

6 **RICHARDS**

5 **LUNDEKVAM**

7 **LE TISSIER**

30 **KACHLOUL**

32 **SOLTVEDT**

8 **OAKLEY**

15 **BENALI**

17 **PAHARS**

9 **HUGHES**

substitutes

35 **BOA MORTE**

16 **BEATTIE**
(for 32) 88 mins

14 **RIPLEY**
(for 7) 53 mins

24 **COLLETER**

13 **MOSS**

Liverpool made a swift return to the Dell, scene of their agonising Worthington Cup exit ten days earlier, and once again it was a stage to forget for Michael Owen. The 19-year-old was switched to the bench by manager Gérard Houllier who opted for a new strike force of Titi Camara and Erik Meijer. And when Owen went on in the second half he lasted just 22 minutes before limping off with a left hamstring problem which would rule him out of the next two matches.

Danny Murphy is determined to get the ball off Matthew Oakley.

1 Liverpool

SCORER: Camara 81

Liverpool's equaliser came when a shot from Jamie Redknapp rebounded off a defender to Titi Camara.

Early in the first half Titi Camara tested Paul Jones when he latched onto Vladimir Smicer's pass and unleashed a 30-yard blast that brought an impressive save from the home goalkeeper.

The roaming, elusive Guinea international continued to torment Southampton. From a Camara pull-back Danny Murphy's sidefoot effort was palmed out by Jones just tantalisingly out of Smicer's reach, while from one of a stream of Steve Staunton crosses Meijer fired over the top of the bar.

Yet despite Liverpool's domination it was Southampton who broke the deadlock six minutes before the half-time interval. Worthington Cup match winner Trond Soltvedt again did the damage with a close range volley from Matt Le Tissier's far post header off Francis Benali's left wing cross.

Just after the introduction of Owen and David Thompson for Meijer and Murphy Liverpool keeper Brad Friedel had to dive to his left to push away a fierce long range shot from Matthew Oakley, following Benali's short free kick.

Soon after Vegard Heggem joined the action, in place of Smicer, the Norwegian headed a long pass from Stephane Henchoz into Owen's path. But the youngster's half volley was too high and things looked bleak for the visitors after Owen's enforced 80th minute exit, leaving Liverpool with ten men.

But little more than a minute later Camara secured a point by letting fly from 20 yards to beat Jones after a Jamie Redknapp shot had rebounded to him off Claus Lundekvam.

While it wasn't exactly a moral victory, Liverpool at least finished on a positive note, having snatched some reward.

FRIEDEL 19
STAUNTON 5
HENCHOZ 2
HYYPIA 12
SONG 4
CARRAGHER 23
MURPHY 24
REDKNAPP 11
SMICER 7
MEIJER 18
CAMARA 22

substitutes
NIELSEN 26
HEGGEM 14
(for 7) 73 mins
MATTEO 21
THOMPSON
(for 24) 58 mins
OWEN 10
(for 18) 58 mins

'Titi Camara's strike was just reward for his endeavour. Camara attempted six shots, completed more than 80 per cent of his passes and ran the Southampton defence ragged at times.' – Liverpool FC Magazine

Liverpool 1

VENUE: Anfield, 7.45pm

ATTENDANCE: 44,012

REFEREE: Stephen Lodge (Barnsley)

SCORER: Camara 43

1 **WESTERVELD**

4 **SONG**

12 **HYYPIA**

21 **MATTEO**

2 **HENCHOZ**

23 **CARRAGHER**

25 **THOMPSON**

11 **REDKNAPP**

15 **BERGER**

22 **CAMARA**

18 **MEIJER**

substitutes

26 **NIELSEN**

14 **HEGGEM**
(for 25) 74 mins

28 **GERRARD**

24 **MURPHY**

7 **SMICER**
(for 22) 79 mins

It was an emotional Anfield evening for crowd favourite Titi Camara who scored the game's only goal within hours of receiving the heartbreaking news of his father Sekou's death. The Guinea striker insisted to manager Gérard Houllier that he wanted to play and proceeded to score his first home goal since his summer move from Marseille, dedicating his 43rd minute strike to the memory of his father, a 62-year-old government ambassador.

Sander Westerveld returned in goal after suspension as one of four changes with Dominic Matteo replacing Steve Staunton at left back, Patrik Berger displacing fellow Czech Vladimir Smicer in midfield and David Thompson coming in for Danny Murphy. West Ham went into the match without the inspirational Paolo Di Canio, and knowing that thay had not won at Anfield for 36 years.

Liverpool quickly gained the initiative in a tight, hard-fought encounter and visiting keeper Shaka Hislop had to tip over a powerful Thompson blast with Erik Meijer and Camara also going close.

But the talents of West Ham's Joe Cole were clearly evident, not least his ability to turn in the smallest of spaces, and his skills demanded constant vigilance from Sami Hyypia, Stephane Henchoz and company.

At the other end, however, in the absence of Michael Owen and Robbie Fowler, the partnership of Camara and Meijer ensured a hard night's work for Anfield 'old boy' Neil Ruddock, Rio Ferdinand and their colleagues. Liverpool persistence was rewarded when Rigobert Song reached the by-line and delivered a cross that embarrassed Ferdinand and fell to Camara to stab in.

Bereaved Camara burst into tears and knelt in prayer after scoring, later saying: 'The goal was for my father. It's thanks to him that I am here today. He told me to go abroad and try to be successful. I told Gérard Houllier I wanted to play for him, for the team and for me.'

Frank Lampard came closest to a second half West Ham goal with a shot from a Joe Cole pull-back. But Westerveld parried the shot and Song cleared the ball hurriedly.

A drained Camara was replaced late in the game by Vladimir Smicer but fittingly, despite further chances at both ends, the African's memorable strike proved decisive and clinched a welcome victory.

> *'I would like to pay special tribute to Titi because today was special for him. I considered leaving him out after he had lost his father. But he told me he wanted to play for his father. The whole team is supporting him and backing him. He was extremely brave.' – Gérard Houllier*

0 West Ham United

HISLOP 1
POTTS 4
FERDINAND 15
RUDDOCK 6
SINCLAIR 8
LAMPARD 18
COLE 26
LOMAS 11
KELLER 7
WANCHOPE 12
KITSON 9

substitutes
FORREST 22
MONCUR 16
FOE 13
MARGAS 30
NEWTON 38

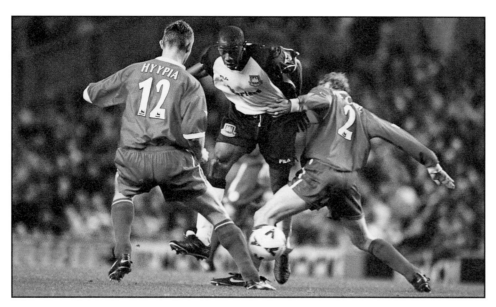

Sami Hyypia and Stephane Henchoz combine to thwart West Ham's Paulo Wanchope.

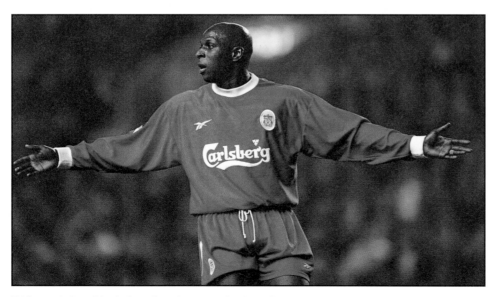

Titi Camara dedicated his winning strike to the memory of his father, Sekou, who died a few hours before the game.

Saturday 2	v	ASTON VILLA	A	0-0
Wednesday 13	v	SOUTHAMPTON	A	1-2
Saturday 16	v	CHELSEA	H	1-0
Saturday 23	v	SOUTHAMPTON	A	1-1
Wednesday 27	v	WEST HAM UNITED	H	1-0

22

TITI CAMARA

PLAYER OF THE MONTH

The former Marseille striker quickly established a warm rapport with Liverpool supporters and struck two precious goals late in the month, firing an equaliser for his ten-man team to earn a point at Southampton and then the winner against West Ham at Anfield.

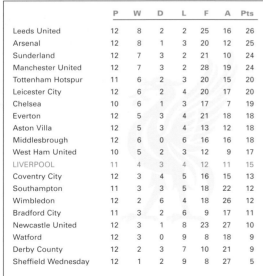

	P	W	D	L	F	A	Pts
Leeds United	12	8	2	2	25	16	26
Arsenal	12	8	1	3	20	12	25
Sunderland	12	7	3	2	21	10	24
Manchester United	12	7	3	2	28	19	24
Tottenham Hotspur	11	6	2	3	20	15	20
Leicester City	12	6	2	4	20	17	20
Chelsea	10	6	1	3	17	7	19
Everton	12	5	3	4	21	18	18
Aston Villa	12	5	3	4	13	12	18
Middlesbrough	12	6	0	6	16	16	18
West Ham United	10	5	2	3	12	9	17
LIVERPOOL	11	4	3	4	12	11	15
Coventry City	12	3	4	5	16	15	13
Southampton	11	3	3	5	18	22	12
Wimbledon	12	2	6	4	18	26	12
Bradford City	11	3	2	6	9	17	11
Newcastle United	12	3	1	8	23	27	10
Watford	12	3	0	9	8	18	9
Derby County	12	2	3	7	10	21	9
Sheffield Wednesday	12	1	2	9	8	27	5

UP TO AND INCLUDING MONDAY 25 OCTOBER 1999

'Talking Points'

- 2/10/99 Liverpool suffered through Robbie Fowler's injury. **Fowler has scored 14 times against Villa**, including 12 in the league.

- 13/10/99 **Michael Owen's goal** against Southampton in the Worthington Cup was his **6th in 8 games** in the competition. It was **his 50th goal for the club in 93 games** in all competitions.

- 16/10/99 **Chelsea have not won at Anfield since 1 February 1992**. Erland Johnsen, Bernard Lambourde and now Desailly and Wise have been sent off at Anfield in recent years.

- 23/10/99 There has been only **one goalless draw** in all league games between **Liverpool and Southampton**.

'Talking Points'

for more info visit www.liverpoolfc.net

november

Monday 1	v	BRADFORD CITY	H
Saturday 6	v	DERBY COUNTY	H
Saturday 20	v	SUNDERLAND	A
Saturday 27	v	WEST HAM UNITED	A

Liverpool | 3

VENUE: Anfield, 8.00pm
ATTENDANCE: 40,483
REFEREE: Jeff Winter (Middlesbrough)

SCORERS: Camara 21
Redknapp 42 (penalty)
Heggem 80

1 **WESTERVELD**
4 **SONG**
12 **HYYPIA**
5 **STAUNTON**
2 **HENCHOZ**
16 **HAMANN**
25 **THOMPSON**
11 **REDKNAPP**
15 **BERGER**
22 **CAMARA**
7 **SMICER**

substitutes

26 **NIELSEN**
14 **HEGGEM**
(for 25) 78 mins
23 **CARRAGHER**
(for 11) 71 mins
24 **MURPHY**
18 **MEIJER**
(for 7) 82 mins

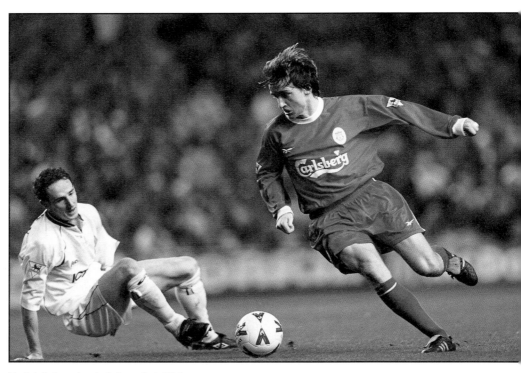

Vladimir Smicer takes the ball past Andy O'Brien.

Liverpool overcame the shock of an early Bradford goal to score three of their own for the first time in the Premiership season, climb above Everton into sixth place and stretch their unbeaten League run to five games.

Dean Windass stunned Anfield with only a dozen minutes on the clock when he fired a Lee Mills pass beyond Sander Westerveld. The shock waves were still reverberating when the Yorkshire visitors, managed by former Liverpool reserve Paul Jewell, should have doubled their lead but Neil Redfearn let Liverpool off the hook by heading over from close range.

But man of the moment Titi Camara, this time partnering Vladimir Smicer up front, put his side level by taking a pass from Steve Staunton – recalled in place of Dominic Matteo – then turning and shooting low past Matt Clarke for his third goal in as many games.

Then, three minutes before the break, Liverpool, who had Dietmar Hamann back in midfield in place of Jamie Carragher after a four-match injury absence, went ahead from the penalty spot after

1 Bradford City

SCORER: Windass 12

Patrik Berger was upended by David Wetherall. Jamie Redknapp drove the spot kick beyond Clarke who distinguished himself in the second half with saves from David Thompson, Berger and Camara.

But Vegard Heggem's introduction for Thompson after 78 minutes produced a quick dividend. The substitute went on a mazy run through the Bradford defence before firing a superb shot past Clarke. But the Bradford goalkeeper prevented his side suffering an even heavier defeat with another great save in the dying seconds by going full length to divert a Camara shot around the post.

> *'Perhaps Paul Jewell should consider himself unlucky that his former club chose to display the attacking prowess which has been buried beneath the surface of more recent workmanlike performances; cutting free from their shackles to clock up an incredible 24 attempts on goal.'*
> – *Paul Joyce,* Liverpool Daily Post

CLARKE 13
HALLE 18
WETHERALL 5
O'BRIEN 14
SHARPE 16
REDFEARN 26
McCALL 4
WINDASS 15
BLAKE 8
SAUNDERS 28
MILLS 9

substitutes
MYERS 3
PRUDHOE 17
DREYER 20
LAWRENCE 7
(for 18) 67 mins
RANKIN 19
(for 26) 79 mins

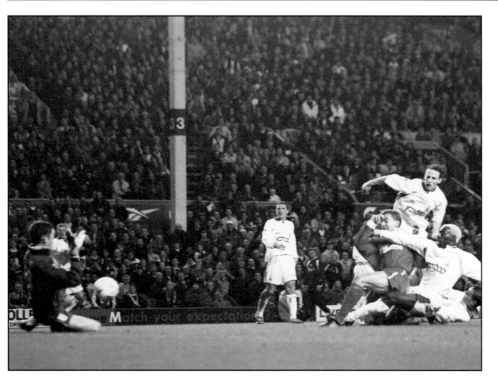

Vegard Heggem ends his second-half run by steering the ball past Bradford's keeper and into the net.

Liverpool 2

VENUE: Anfield, 3.00pm

ATTENDANCE: 44,467

REFEREE: Uriah Rennie (Sheffield)

SCORERS: Murphy 65
Redknapp 69

1 **WESTERVELD**

14 **HEGGEM**

12 **HYYPIA**

5 **STAUNTON**

2 **HENCHOZ**

16 **HAMANN**

23 **CARRAGHER**

11 **REDKNAPP**

10 **OWEN**

22 **CAMARA**

7 **SMICER**

substitutes

26 **NIELSEN**

28 **GERRARD**
(for 10) 80 mins

25 **THOMPSON**

24 **MURPHY**
(for 7) 15 mins

18 **MEIJER**
(for 22) 56 mins

A battling performance in a hard-fought contest secured maximum reward for Liverpool, their victory clinched by two second half goals in a four-minute span from Danny Murphy and Jamie Redknapp that took them into fifth place.

Manager Gérard Houllier restored Michael Owen to the starting line-up along with Vegard Heggem and Jamie Carragher with David Thompson reverting to the bench and flu-hit Patrik Berger and hamstring casualty Rigobert Song absent.

And Liverpool were hit by more injury setbacks during the game. Vladimir Smicer pulled up with a hamstring problem which sent Murphy into the fray as the Czech's replacement after only 15 minutes. Then, with the game still goalless, Titi Camara limped off with thigh damage in the second half with Erik Meijer going on.

Danny Murphy smashes the ball off Prior's leg to give the Reds a 65th-minute lead.

Camara excited the crowd with an early overhead effort from Owen's cross which flew over the Derby bar before a rasping Carragher drive from 20 yards went even closer to counting.

> *'Liverpool underlined they have learned one lesson in the year Gérard Houllier has been boss... scrapping for a win from an indifferent display. He has instilled a resilience and concentration that is helping the team dig out results.'* – Richard Tanner, Sunday Express

0 Derby County

Sami Hyypia, whose 20th-minute tussle with Stefano Eranio led to Derby's Italian midfielder being stretchered off with a broken leg, rescued Liverpool by blocking Deon Burton's shot on the line. After Redknapp had fired wide Derby threatened again just before the interval. But Rory Delap's shot was diverted for a corner and early in the second half Murphy made a goal-line clearance from substitute Spencer Prior's powerful header.

Murphy and Prior figured again shortly afterwards in the moment that broke the deadlock after 65 minutes. Murphy, sent away by Meijer, worked space for himself and unleashed a fierce shot that deflected wickedly off Prior past goalkeeper Russell Hoult, the FA's Dubious Goals Committee confirming Murphy as the scorer of his first League goal for the club.

Liverpool swiftly wrapped up victory when Redknapp, looking offside, was allowed to chase Steve Staunton's through ball and when the advancing Hoult fluffed his attempted clearance the Anfield skipper gleefully slotted his shot into an unguarded net. Steven Gerrard was a late substitute for Owen, who headed off to play in England's Euro 2000 play-offs against Scotland.

For Liverpool it was another three valuable points.

HOULT 1
CARBONARI 2
SCHNOOR 3
POWELL 4
DORIGO 5
JOHNSON 7
BURTON 9
DELAP 10
LAURSEN 16
FUERTES 20
ERANIO 29

substitutes
PRIOR 17
(for 7) 51 mins
STURRIDGE 8
(for 20) 51 mins
BORBOKIS 22
(for 29) 20 mins
CHRISTIE 12
KNIGHT 32

Steve Staunton delivers a pinpoint cross despite the attention of two Derby defenders.

Sunderland | 0

VENUE: Stadium of Light, 3.00pm

ATTENDANCE: 42,015

REFEREE: Dermot Gallagher (Banbury)

1 **SORENSEN**

18 **WILLIAMS**

17 **CRADDOCK**

6 **BUTLER**

3 **GRAY**

7 **SUMMERBEE**

29 **ROY**

16 **RAE**

21 **McCANN**

9 **QUINN**

10 **PHILLIPS**

substitutes

13 **MARRIOTT**

14 **HOLLOWAY**

15 **FREDGAARO**

19 **THIRLWELL**

31 **REDDY**
(for 16) 84 mins

A superb goal from Michael Owen was the perfect reply to critics of his England Euro 2000 play-off displays against Scotland and set Liverpool on the road to their fourth straight Premiership win.

A late strike from Patrik Berger ensured the continuation of Liverpool's unbeaten away record at Sunderland stretching back to 1958 and at the same time inflicted the Wearside's club's first defeat for a year at the Stadium of Light.

In a forgettable, low-tempo opening half the recalled Rigobert Song cleared off the line from Niall Quinn after the big Ireland striker had beaten Sami Hyypia and fired over the diving Sander Westerveld.

> *'That was a fantastic result, as good a one as I've seen since I have been at Liverpool. We battled so well and we're going the right way. Maybe a few years ago we'd have lost games like that. But we're all together, we're pulling in the right direction and enjoying our football.'*
> – Jamie Redknapp

Michael Owen squeezes past Sunderland's Summerbee and Williams.

2 | *Liverpool*

SCORERS: Owen 63

Berger 85

Liverpool survived another scare soon after the interval when Kevin Phillips spurned a close range chance by heading wide from Nicky Summerbee's cross.

But Owen, playing as a lone attacker just in front of Danny Murphy and a midfield that had Steven Gerrard as well as Berger back in its ranks, put Liverpool ahead with a memorable 62nd minute strike. He seized on Hyypia's long pass, shrugged off the snapping attentions of Jody Craddock and despite being off balance lofted the ball over Thomas Sorensen for a goal that would have been beyond the ambit of many forwards.

Five minutes from time David Thompson, a late substitiute for Gerrard, pulled the ball back from the by-line for Berger to fire home right-footed past diving Sorensen.

'There's been a lot of criticism of the team and certain individuals recently so it was nice to silence the critics,' said Owen. 'If I was celebrating aferwards it's because winning and doing well for Liverpool means a lot to me.'

The satisfaction for manager Gérard Houllier was over his team's harvest of maximum points from their last four games.

WESTERVELD 1

HYYPIA 12

HENCHOZ 2

MATTEO 21

SONG 4

GERRARD 28

MURPHY 24

REDKNAPP 11

BERGER 15

HAMANN 16

OWEN 10

substitutes

FRIEDEL 19

HEGGEM 14
(for 10) 90 mins

TRAORE 30

THOMPSON
(for 28) 81 mins

MEIJER 18
(for 24) 74 mins

Danny Murphy retains his balance despite having his shirt tugged by Sunderland's Darren Williams.

West Ham United 1

VENUE: Upton Park, 3.00pm

ATTENDANCE: 26,043

REFEREE: Graham Barber (Tring)

SCORER: Sinclair 45

1 **HISLOP**

15 **FERDINAND**

6 **RUDDOCK**

30 **MARGAS**

7 **KELLER**

11 **LOMAS**

8 **SINCLAIR**

18 **LAMPARD**

26 **COLE**

10 **DI CANIO**

12 **WANCHOPE**

substitutes

22 **FORREST**

13 **FOE**

16 **MONCUR**

4 **POTTS**

9 **KITSON**
(for 12) 77 mins

Liverpool's unbeaten run ended in disappointment and controversy at Upton Park where they slipped to their first defeat in eight Premiership games.

At the end of the first half there were strong appeals for a penalty from Liverpool players when Michael Owen went down in the box under a challenge from former Anfield defender Neil Ruddock.

David Thompson tussles with West Ham's Joe Cole.

> *'For a young lad, and with the physique he has, Michael Owen gets pushed a lot and faces a lot of physical toughness. He withstands that very well. He's very quick so when he turns players either he gets through or he falls.*
>
> *'I don't think he dived. If you can't protect the strikers we have a problem in football.'* – Gérard Houllier

0 Liverpool

But referee Graham Barber rejected the claims and booked Owen for diving. But worse was to come for Liverpool, who were captained by Sami Hyypia in the absence of Jamie Redknapp, whose cartilage damage required surgery that would keep him out for four months.

With seconds of the opening period remaining Steve Lomas set up what was to prove West Ham's winner. His cross from the right was met by Paolo Di Danio and although Sander Westerveld stopped the Italian's shot Trevor Sinclair swooped on the rebound to score.

Patrik Berger does his best to tackle West Ham's scorer Trevor Sinclair.

WESTERVELD 1
SONG 4
HENCHOZ 2
HYYPIA 12
MATTEO 21
HEGGEM 14
HAMANN 16
GERRARD 28
BERGER 15
MURPHY 24
OWEN 10

substitutes
FRIEDEL 19
STAUNTON 5
(for 10) 75 mins
CARRAGHER 23
THOMPSON 25
(for 15) 16 mins
MEIJER 18
(for 4) 70 mins

Liverpool thought they had equalised early in the second half when Owen netted from a header by David Thompson, a first half replacement for knee casualty Patrik Berger. But Owen's effort was disallowed because Rigobert Song's original cross had gone out of play.

Thompson went close to levelling the scoreline when his shot from Danny Murphy's pass beat Shaka Hislop but, agonisingly for Liverpool, just beat the upright, too.

Gérard Houllier sent on Erik Meijer for Song for the final 20 minutes and soon after Steve Staunton replaced a limping, cramp-hit Owen. Liverpool had a let off when Paulo Wanchope fired over from point blank range after Di Canio's header crashed off a post and rebounded to the Costa Rican forward.

At the other end Steven Gerrard headed over from a Staunton cross while the game ended with more bewitching skill from Di Canio who set up a chance for Joe Cole, from which the youngster fired too high.

Monday 1	v	BRADFORD CITY	H	3-1	
Saturday 6	v	DERBY COUNTY	H	2-0	
Saturday 20	v	SUNDERLAND	A	2-0	
Saturday 27	v	WEST HAM UNITED	A	0-1	

12

SAMI HYYPIA

PLAYER OF THE MONTH

The displays of centre back Hyypia, the giant Finn who became an instant favourite with the Kop, were recognised when he was named Carling Player of the Month for November, a month in which he took on the added responsibility of the captaincy after Jamie Redknapp's knee injury. Hyypia was also honoured by being named Finland's Player of the Year.

	P	W	D	L	F	A	Pts
Leeds United	16	11	2	3	29	19	35
Manchester United	15	10	3	2	35	20	33
Arsenal	16	10	2	4	28	16	32
Sunderland	16	9	4	3	27	16	31
Leicester City	16	9	2	5	26	20	29
LIVERPOOL	16	8	3	5	20	13	27
Tottenham Hotspur	15	8	2	5	25	20	26
Chelsea	14	7	3	4	20	11	24
West Ham United	15	7	3	5	17	14	24
Middlesbrough	16	7	2	7	20	23	23
Everton	16	5	6	5	24	22	21
Coventry City	16	5	5	6	23	18	20
Aston Villa	16	5	4	7	14	18	19
Wimbledon	16	3	8	5	22	29	17
Newcastle United	16	4	4	8	27	30	16
Southampton	15	4	4	7	20	25	16
Bradford City	15	3	3	9	12	24	12
Derby County	16	3	3	10	15	28	12
Watford	16	3	2	11	13	28	11
Sheffield Wednesday	15	1	3	11	13	36	6

UP TO AND INCLUDING SUNDAY 28 NOVEMBER 1999

'Talking Points'

- 6/11/99 Derby have **won only once at Anfield** since 1969–70. That came in 1998–99.

- 6/11/99 In the game against Derby, **Danny Murphy scored his first League goal** for Liverpool.

- 20/11/99 **Liverpool inflicted Sunderland's first defeat** at the Stadium of Light this season.

- 20/11/99 **Sunderland have not beaten Liverpool** at home **since August 1958**. **Liverpool** have **won 12** and **drawn 6** of the ensuing 18 visits to Sunderland.

- 27/11/99 **Jamie Redknapp** has yet to score in the eight games he has played against his father's club.

'Talking Points'

for more info visit www.liverpoolfc.net

december

Sunday 5	v	SHEFFIELD WEDNESDAY	H
Sunday 12	v	HUDDERSFIELD TOWN	A
Saturday 18	v	COVENTRY CITY	H
Sunday 26	v	NEWCASTLE UNITED	A
Tuesday 28	v	WIMBLEDON	H

Liverpool | 4

VENUE: Anfield, 4.00pm
ATTENDANCE: 42,517
REFEREE: Paul Durkin (Portland)

SCORERS: Hyypia 21
Murphy 41
Gerrard 69
Thompson 79

1 **WESTERVELD**
4 **SONG**
12 **HYYPIA**
21 **MATTEO**
2 **HENCHOZ**
16 **HAMANN**
25 **THOMPSON**
28 **GERRARD**
24 **MURPHY**
10 **OWEN**
22 **CAMARA**

substitutes

19 **FRIEDEL**
23 **CARRAGHER**
(for 4) 73 mins
5 **STAUNTON**
(for 24) 75 mins
18 **MEIJER**
9 **FOWLER**
(for 10) 81 mins

Liverpool recovered from a spectacular first half Wednesday strike to plunder some memorable goals of their own, capped by the late bonus of Robbie Fowler's long awaited return.

Victory lifted Liverpool to fifth place but they had to overcome the shock of a magnificent 20-yard, 18th-minute strike by Niclas Alexandersson that put the rock-bottom visitors ahead and survive some other scares before taking control. Acting skipper Sami Hyypia swiftly levelled the score when he powered in a header from a corner by David Thompson, who had come in for knee casualty Patrik Berger with Titi Camara's return alongside Michael Owen squeezing Vegard Heggem out of the re-shaped side.

Shortly before the interval Danny Murphy put Liverpool ahead when he pounced on the rebound after Wednesday goalkeeper Kevin Pressman had superbly kept out a fierce dipping Thompson volley following a Rigobert Song throw-in.

Scorers Danny Murphy and Niclas Alexandersson in a race for possession.

1 Sheffield Wednesday

SCORER: Alexandersson 18

Yet still Wednesday had chances, one of them bizarrely created by Owen's slip that let in Alexandersson. This time the Swede's shot through a ruck of players was well saved by Sander Westerveld. The Wednesday raider had yet another, clearer opportunity but spurned it by firing wide.

With 20 minutes left though, Steven Gerrard hit a wonderful first senior goal for Liverpool. Seizing on a Song pass the 19-year-old ran head-on at Wednesday's defence, feinted to shoot and then drifted past Emerson Thome and Des Walker to dispatch a brilliant right-foot shot past Pressman. The lively, industrious Thompson then put the icing on Liverpool's cake by cutting in from the right and tormenting the Wednesday rearguard before bending a left-foot effort into the net.

> *'The manager tells us every day in training to keep our feet on the ground. He's been fantastic. He's given us all our chance and we're paying him back for that.'*
> – Sky TV Man of the Match, David Thompson

With nine minutes left manager Gérard Houllier sent on Fowler in place of Owen for his first senior action after missing 12 of the previous 13 games with ankle damage.

PRESSMAN 1
NOLAN 17
THOME 5
WALKER 6
BRISCOE 21
ALEXANDERSSON 16
ATHERTON 2
JONK 4
RUDI 14
BOOTH 10
DE BILDE 23

substitutes
SIBON 9
(for 21) 81 mins
CRESSWELL 12
(for 23) 78 mins
QUINN 33
(for 14) 90 mins
HASLAM 22
SRNICEK 28

Left: Danny Murphy celebrates putting the Reds into the lead.

Far left: Wednesday keeper Pressman grabs the ball off Michael Owen's foot.

Huddersfield Town | 0

VENUE: McAlpine Stadium, 2.00pm
ATTENDANCE: 23,678
REFEREE: Rob Harris (Oxford)

'It was an education for some of our younger players and also the foreign ones. What I liked was that they were disciplined and are improving by the game. I'm happy Dominic scored and proved it's not just about the 11 who start.' – Gérard Houllier

1 **VAESEN**
2 **JENKINS**
3 **VINCENT**
4 **ARMSTRONG**
12 **THORNLEY**
6 **GRAY**
40 **GORRE**
8 **IRONS**
9 **STEWART**
10 **SELLARS**
11 **WIJNHARD**

substitutes

13 **MARGETSON**
21 **DYSON**
14 **HORNE**
7 **DONIS**
(for 12) 70 mins
25 **SCHOFIELD**
(for 9) 82 mins

Titi Camara continued his great run of goals with a strike late in the first half.

Liverpool opened their FA Cup campaign under fierce home pressure but punctured the giant-killing ambitions of their First Division foes with goals in each half from Titi Camara and Dominic Matteo.

The visit to the McAlpine Stadium was a notable milestone for Michael Owen, his 100th Liverpool appearance in his last game as a teenager two days before his 20th birthday.

He missed out on celebrating with a goal, first finding himself blocked by Jamie Vincent and then seeing his shot after an explosive run beaten away by home keeper Nico Vaesen.

But Owen's attack partner Camara came up with a timely strike late in the first half after Huddersfield had failed to take several chances with Clyde Wijnhard firing wide and having another shot saved by Sander Westerveld who dealt likewise with a Kenny Irons effort and a fierce drive from Ben Thornley.

Camara's breakthrough was set-up by Vladimir Smicer, who was restored after injury in place of the suspended David Thompson with Steven Gerrard at right back in place of Rigobert Song and Jamie Carragher recalled to midfield.

From fit-again Smicer's cross Camara, managing to elude the entire home defence, smashed a magnificent shot past the helpless Vaesen. Wijnhard was again off target with a shot and a header either side of half time and Liverpool clinched victory just before the hour mark.

2 Liverpool

SCORERS: **Camara 36**
Matteo 59

This time Camara turned provider by linking with Smicer and delivering a precise crossfield pass into the path of Dominic Matteo, who had replaced injured Steve Staunton in the first half. The left back advanced for some 30 yards before firing past Vaesen for only the second goal of his Liverpool career to secure the club's fourth round place.

With three minutes left Jon Newby, who had made his debut as a Worthington Cup substitute against Hull in September, got a taste of FA Cup action in place of Gerrard.

This was a worthy win by Liverpool in what was a potential banana-skin cup tie.

Dominic Matteo is engulfed by team-mates after scoring only the second goal of his Liverpool career.

WESTERVELD 1
HYYPIA 12
HENCHOZ 2
STAUNTON 5
CARRAGHER 23
SMICER 7
MURPHY 24
GERRARD 28
HAMANN 16
CAMARA 22
OWEN 10

substitutes
FRIEDEL 19
MATTEO 21
(for 5) 35 mins
SONG 4
(for 7) 70 mins
NEWBY 32
(for 28) 88 mins
MEIJER 18

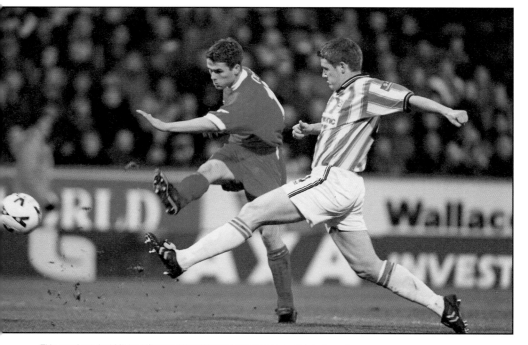
This match marked Michael Owen's 100th Liverpool appearance, and his last as a teenager.

Liverpool 2

VENUE: **Anfield, 3.00pm**

ATTENDANCE: **44,024**

REFEREE: **Andy D'Urso (Billericay)**

SCORERS: **Owen 45**

Camara 74

1 **WESTERVELD**

12 **HYYPIA**

21 **MATTEO**

2 **HENCHOZ**

23 **CARRAGHER**

16 **HAMANN**

25 **THOMPSON**

28 **GERRARD**

15 **BERGER**

10 **OWEN**

22 **CAMARA**

substitutes

26 **NIELSEN**

4 **SONG**

14 **HEGGEM**
(for 7) 85 mins

24 **MURPHY**
(for 7) 88 mins

7 **SMICER**
(for 25) 35 mins

There was an emotional, carnival atmosphere at Anfield to celebrate the 40th anniversary of the late Bill Shankly's first match in charge of Liverpool: 19 December 1959. A Scottish piper played 'Amazing Grace', the Kop sang 'You'll Never Walk Alone' and great players of yesteryear walked onto the turf to pay their own tribute to a man who, by common consent, is hailed as the founding inspiration of the modern Liverpool. The parade of former stars included Ron Yeats, Willie Stevenson, Tommy Lawrence, Tommy Smith, Ian St John, Gerry Byrne, Gordon Milne, Peter Thompson, Brian Hall and England manager Kevin Keegan who declared: 'Shankly changed my life and I miss him.

'Everything I see here today may have been down to a lot of people but nobody will disagree that the man who deserves most credit was Bill Shankly.'

Keegan was also an admirer of the way his England striker Michael Owen, with his back to goal, seized on Dominic Matteo's pass in first half stoppage time, turned Gary Breen and and beat Magnus Hedman for his first home goal of the season.

Vladimir Smicer and Paul Telfer tussle for possession.

0 Coventry City

Shankly would have appreciated that moment of sheer class to end an opening period which had seen chances at both ends and a controversial moment when Coventry boss Gordon Strachan leapt from the directors box into the crowd to get to the touchline after Breen had been booked following a tussle with Owen.

'He just came down to wish me a merry Christmas,' quipped Strachan's counterpart Gérard Houllier, who had the satisfaction of

HEDMAN 1

TELFER 12

BREEN 17

WILLIAMS 4

FROGGATT 16

CHIPPO 18

PALMER 14

McALLISTER 10

HADJI 11

WHELAN 8

KEANE 7

substitutes

NORMANN 20
(for 11) 75 mins

ROUSSEL 31
(for 8) 70 mins

EUSTACE 24

OGRIZOVIC 26

GUSTAFSON 32

'Michael said my shot hit him on the back but it's definitely my goal. It's one of the best I've scored. The supporters have been fantastic to me here. It's amazing how they have taken to me in my first season and that's why I want to give 200 per cent on the pitch.' – Titi Camara

---

seeing Titi Camara, again partnering Owen in the absence of ankle casualty Fowler, score his seventh goal of the season.

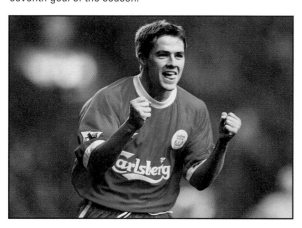

Sander Westerveld protected his side's lead with saves from Carlton Palmer and Noel Whelan before Camara clinched victory by conjuring something from nothing as he wheeled onto Dominic Matteo's throw on the left and unleashed a 25-yard blast that deflected off Owen's back into the top corner of Hedman's Kop net.

Shankly would have applauded that one, too.

Top: Dietmar Hamann rides a tough challenge from Carlton Palmer.

Left: Michael Owen is pleased with his seventh goal of the season.

Newcastle United | 2

VENUE: St James Park, 3.00pm

ATTENDANCE: 36,445

REFEREE: David Elleray (Harrow-on-the-Hill)

SCORERS: Shearer 12
Ferguson 67

13 **HARPER**

2 **BARTON**

18 **HUGHES**

34 **DABIZAS**

36 **PISTONE**

7 **DYER**

11 **SPEED**

37 **LEE**

15 **SOLANO**

20 **FERGUSON**

9 **SHEARER**

substitutes

1 **GIVEN**

3 **MARCELINO**

17 **GLASS**
(for 7) 53 mins

32 **GALLACHER**
(for 15) 73 mins

14 **KETSBAIA**
(for 20) 90 mins

Two-goal Michael Owen was the star of a contest bristling with scoring opportunites to delight Anfield boss Gérard Houllier and again impress watching England manager Kevin Keegan.

Liverpool were without the considerable presence of Stephane Henchoz, whose increasingly influential centre back partnership with Sami Hyypia was disrupted at St James' Park because of the Swiss defender's one-match suspension. It meant Jamie Carragher switching to the heart of defence and Steven Gerrard into midfield against a Newcastle side showing clear signs of recovery under Bobby Robson's management and fresh from a 6-1 FA Cup hammering of Tottenham .

The attacking nature of the contest was signalled with only four minutes on the clock when Owen found himself deemed onside as he ran clear. But before he could shoot he was robbed by a last-ditch Warren Barton tackle.

Dominic Matteo evades the challenge of Nolberto Solano.

2 Liverpool

SCORER: Owen 31, 53

It was Newcastle, though, who broke the deadlock when Nolberto Solano's right-flank free kick, awarded for Danny Murphy's challenge on Gary Speed, took the merest of glances off Alan Shearer's head to nestle in Sander Westerveld's net.

> *'For Liverpool's first goal we had two defenders and the goalkeeper against Owen and he was too good for the three of us. His second was a present. But again he took it brilliantly and it wasn't an easy chance. He's shown what a great little finisher he is.'*
> *– Newcastle manager Bobby Robson*

Home keeper Steve Harper saved from Titi Camara and Patrik Berger, both from moves launched by former Newcastle midfielder Dietmar Hamann, before Owen equalised. From Camara's pass Owen delightfully tricked his way past Aaron Hughes and Alessandro Pistone to beat Harper with a right foot angled shot. Newcastle responded with a long range Barton effort tipped over by Westerveld and a Speed header wastefully wide before Owen struck again early in the second half by converting an underhit Nikos Dabizas back pass.

But Liverpool were denied victory by their former Mersey derby adversary Duncan Ferguson, the one-time Everton striker equalising with a diving header off Barton's high cross. With seven minutes left Robbie Fowler, who had again been hit by ankle damage, returned as substitute for Danny Murphy.

But it was Newcastle who finished the stronger, spurred on by Ferguson's equaliser, and Liverpool were content to share the Christmas spoils.

WESTERVELD 1
SONG 4
HYYPIA 12
CARRAGHER 23
MATTEO 21
MURPHY 24
GERRARD 28
HAMANN 16
BERGER 15
OWEN 10
CAMARA 22

substitutes

FOWLER 9
(for 24) 82 mins

HEGGEM 14
(for 22) 69 mins

FRIEDEL 19

TRAORE 30

STAUNTON 5

Titi Camara indulges in some impromptu arm wrestling with Nikos Dabizas.

Liverpool | 3

VENUE: Anfield, 3.00pm
ATTENDANCE: 44,107
REFEREE: Neale Barry (Scunthorpe)

SCORER: Owen 58
Berger 68
Fowler 80

1 **WESTERVELD**
28 **GERRARD**
2 **HENCHOZ**
12 **HYYPIA**
21 **MATTEO**
14 **HEGGEM**
23 **CARRAGHER**
24 **MURPHY**
15 **BERGER**
10 **OWEN**
22 **CAMARA**

substitutes

5 **STAUNTON**
26 **NIELSEN**
9 **FOWLER**
(for 24) 58
7 **SMICER**
(for 10) 65
4 **SONG**
(for 22) 89

Sami Hyypia rises above the Wimbledon defence only for Sullivan to make a save.

Injury-haunted Robbie Fowler rose from the substitute's bench to clinch victory for Liverpool with his 150th career goal in Anfield's final match of the old millennium.

To emphasise the scale of Gérard Houllier's squad rebuilding the Liverpool team – which had Stephane Henchoz back after suspension but was stripped of flu victim Dietmar Hamann – included only three players, Jamie Carragher, Dominic Matteo and Patrik Berger, who had lined up against Wimbledon in the final game of the previous season.

But some things never change, including Wimbledon's penchant for making life difficult for Liverpool. While lacking in attacking threat themselves the unfashionable visitors made Houllier's side battle hard to find a way through. In the first half they were often caught offside by the Dons, whose goalkeeper Neil Sullivan dealt comfortably with shots from Michael Owen and Titi Camara. Sullivan denied Sami Hyypia after the interval before Michael Owen broke the stalemate by meeting Danny Murphy's corner and steering the ball into the roof of the net. It was Owen's fourth goal in three games and eighth of the season and was immediately followed by Fowler's entrance in place of Murphy.

1 | Wimbledon

SCORER: Gayle 64

Typically, though, Wimbledon levelled when Marcus Gayle evaded the defence, met Kenny Cunningham's cross and directed a downward header past Sander Westerveld. Hamstring casualty Owen then limped off to be replaced by Vladimir Smicer.

Owen's exit meant that he and fellow England striker Fowler had played just 104 minutes together so far in the season underlining Houllier's claim that his side had been robbed of vast scoring potency.

> *'Because of my injuries and the time I've been out my 150th goal has been a long time coming. I don't score too many with my head and I was pleased to see it go in, particularly as I'd connected with the ball on the edge of the box in front of the Kop. There seemed to be 40,000 people willing it go in.' – Robbie Fowler*

But just when Wimbledon were thinking they might escape with a point Berger took full advantage of Hermann Hreidarsson's handling offence on the edge of the box by smashing in a free kick that Sullivan never even saw.

And Fowler, from Smicer's flick, secured victory with a long, looping header to mark his 261st Liverpool appearance with his 150th goal and Liverpool's last of a century they had dominated with 18 championships, four European Cups, five FA Cups, two UEFA Cups and five League Cup triumphs.

It was a certainly a satisfying way to end the old millennium and the young Liverpool team now faced the footballing challenges of the 21st century.

SULLIVAN 1
CUNNINGHAM 2
KIMBLE 3
THATCHER 6
EARLE 8
EUELL 10
GAYLE 11
LEABURN 15
BADIR 19
ANDERSEN 29
HREIDARSSON 30

substitutes
CORT 7
(for 3) 34 mins
ANDRESEN 20
(for 15) 65 mins
FRANCIS 24
(for 19) 77 mins
HEALD 13
WILLMOTT 22

Top: Robbie Fowler celebrates his important 80th-minute strike.

Left: Berger's precise free kick gave Sullivan no chance.

Sunday 5	v	SHEFFIELD WEDNESDAY	H	4-1
Sunday 12	v	HUDDERSFIELD TOWN	A	2-0
Saturday 18	v	COVENTRY CITY	H	2-0
Sunday 26	v	NEWCASTLE UNITED	A	2-2
Tuesday 28	v	WIMBLEDON	H	3-1

M

GERARD HOULLIER

MAN OF THE MONTH

His side's performances during December, in which they won three and drew one of four Premiership games and won an FA Cup tie at Huddersfield, earned the Liverpool boss the Carling Manager of the Month award. 'Awards like this are to be shared with the team and the team behind the team,' said Houllier. 'It is because the players have shown the right attitude, and also because I am receiving great support from the backroom staff.'

	P	W	D	L	F	A	Pts
Leeds United	19	14	2	3	34	20	44
Manchester United	18	13	3	2	48	23	42
Sunderland	19	11	4	4	33	22	37
Arsenal	19	11	3	5	34	20	36
LIVERPOOL	19	10	4	5	28	16	34
Tottenham Hotspur	18	9	3	6	30	22	30
Leicester City	19	9	2	8	27	26	29
Everton	19	7	6	6	33	28	27
Chelsea	17	8	3	6	23	18	27
Middlesbrough	19	8	3	8	23	26	27
West Ham United	18	7	5	6	21	20	26
Aston Villa	19	7	4	8	18	20	25
Coventry City	19	6	6	7	26	22	24
Wimbledon	19	4	10	5	30	32	22
Newcastle United	19	5	5	9	30	34	20
Southampton	18	4	5	9	21	29	17
Bradford City	18	4	4	10	15	29	16
Derby County	19	4	3	12	16	31	15
Watford	19	3	2	14	14	40	11
Sheffield Wednesday	18	2	3	13	16	42	9

UP TO AND INCLUDING SUNDAY 26 DECEMBER 1999

'Talking Points'

- 5/12/99 **Not one of the games** between Liverpool and Sheffield Wednesday at Anfield has been goalless.

- 12/12/99 **Michael Owen made his 100th appearance** for the club. He'd scored **51 goals** in those appearances. **Robbie Fowler** had scored **51 goals in his first 99 appearances**, but in his 100th game he **scored 4 times** against Bolton.

- 12/12/99 **Titi Camara scored on his FA Cup debut** v Huddersfield. **Steven Gerrard, Dietmar Hamann, Stephane Henchoz, Sami Hyypia, Jon Newby and Sander Westerveld all made FA Cup debuts** for the club against Huddersfield Town, **as did Smicer and Song.**

'Talking Points'

for more info visit www.liverpoolfc.net

january

Monday 3	v	TOTTENHAM HOTSPUR	A
Monday 10	v	BLACKBURN ROVERS	H
Saturday 15	v	WATFORD	A
Saturday 22	v	MIDDLESBROUGH	H

Tottenham Hotspur | 1

VENUE: White Hart Lane, 3.00pm

ATTENDANCE: 36,044

REFEREE: Alan Wilkie (Chester-le-Street)

SCORER: Armstrong 23

1 **WALKER**
2 **CARR**
5 **CAMPBELL**
6 **PERRY**
21 **YOUNG**
3 **TARICCO**
25 **CLEMENCE**
8 **SHERWOOD**
14 **GINOLA**
16 **ARMSTRONG**
10 **IVERSEN**

substitutes

13 **BAARDSEN**
7 **ANDERTON**
15 **VEGA**
20 **DOMINGUEZ**
27 **GOWER**

Liverpool's first action of the 21st century brought their first defeat in six league and Cup games and only their second in 13 Premiership outings. Chris Armstrong's goal left Liverpool without a win in London for two seasons. The disappointment for manager Gérard Houllier went beyond his team's below-par performance and the absence of Michael Owen and Robbie Fowler with respective hamstring and ankle problems as well as knee casualty Jamie Redknapp and calf victim Erik Meijer.

He also saw Titi Camara collect a second half booking which meant the Guinea striker would be banned for the forthcoming match against Middlesbrough.

Armstrong had already spurned two chances, both created by David Ginola, before the former Wrexham forward's decisive 23rd minute strike. From 25 yards range he latched onto Vegard Heggem's attempted headed clearance and lashed a shot into the top corner of Sander Westerveld's net.

A few minutes later Tottenham had the ball in the Liverpool net again but Sol Campbell's header from Ginola's free kick was ruled out for offside. The best of Liverpool's first half chances fell to Camara but his shot was saved by Ian Walker with Steven Gerrard putting a follow-up effort into the side netting.

Westerveld, who was Liverpool's best player, saved from both Ginola and Steffen Iversen with

Dominic Matteo rises to head the ball clear from Steffen Iversen.

Armstrong going close to conjuring a second home goal when his off-target shot deflected off Stephane Henchoz almost into his own net.

In the second half Liverpool improved but still struggled to create chances. Vladimir Smicer,

0 Liverpool

Sami Hyypia makes sure that there's no way through for Stephen Clemence.

WESTERVELD 1
HEGGEM 14
HYYPIA 12
HENCHOZ 2
MATTEO 21
SMICER 7
HAMANN 16
CARRAGHER 23
GERRARD 28
BERGER 15
CAMARA 22

substitutes
NIELSEN 26
SONG 4
STAUNTON 5
(for 7) 81 mins
MURPHY 24
(for 15) 73 mins
THOMPSON 25
(for 23) 58 mins

chosen as Camara's attack partner, had one shot saved by Walker and saw another curl wide. But it was a lacklustre Liverpool display on a day when a three-goal win could have lifted them to third place. By unhappy coincidence the scoreline was identical to their opening match of the 20th century… Sunderland 1 Liverpool 0, on 1 January 1900.

'I didn't recognise my team, especially in the first half. We lacked a bit of character that we normally show. We improved in the second half but it was not enough. I have to admit that maybe Tottenham wanted to win more than us. You have to hold up your hands and say it was not our day.' – Gérard Houllier

Liverpool | 0

VENUE: Anfield, 8.00pm

ATTENDANCE: 32,839

REFEREE: Graham Poll (Tring)

1 **WESTERVELD**

28 **GERRARD**

2 **HENCHOZ**

12 **HYYPIA**

21 **MATTEO**

7 **SMICER**

23 **CARRAGHER**

16 **HAMANN**

15 **BERGER**

22 **CAMARA**

24 **MURPHY**

substitutes

32 **NEWBY**
(for 23) 89 mins

25 **THOMPSON**
(for 24) 57 mins

26 **NIELSEN**

14 **HEGGEM**

5 **STAUNTON**

A stunning classic counter-punch crushed Liverpool's FA Cup ambitions and completed a remarkable hat-trick of lower division Anfield 'B stings' in seven years.

'It's a major setback but we have to live with it,' said manager Gérard Houllier after a contest in which Liverpool dominated possession but saw the First Division visitors give a disciplined, determined display and dramatically snatch victory with six minutes left.

Damien Duff sent Per Frandsen attacking down the right and when the Dane's pass found Nathan Blake in yards of space the Wales striker, who shrugged off a hamstring problem to play in the tie, steered a curling shot over Sander Westerveld. It was a goal that shocked home fans and sent visiting supporters into ecstasy. After all, under the guidance of Tony Parkes their team had been 8-1 against to secure a fifth round clash with Newcastle. 'As an individual result it's the best I've had,' Parkes enthused. 'Winning at Anfield takes some doing.'

Centre back Sami Hyypia had an early opportunity to put Liverpool on course to confirming the bookmakers' odds but his header from Patrik Berger's free kick went straight into the clutches of John Filan. The Australian goalkeeper later also denied Danny Murphy with his leg in a one-to-one duel with the recalled player, who was partnering Titi Camara up front in the continued absence of injured strikers Michael Owen, Robbie Fowler and Erik Meijer.

Although Liverpool dominated the early stages of the second half, their lack of a cutting edge proved their undoing. But Blackburn, on the stage where the Ewood Park club had celebrated their championship triumph less than five years earlier, responded with a superb four-man move which ended with Blake demanding a fine save from Westerveld, who also denied Simon Grayson.

Liverpool's anxieties grew as Filan made second half stops from Camara and Vladimir Smicer before a Dominic Matteo shot was deflected for a corner. Then came Blackburn's decisive break to become only the third lower division club in 36 years to eliminate Liverpool from the FA Cup at Anfield. The names of the other two, both in the 1990s, also began with a 'B' ... Bolton and Bristol City.

> *'Liverpool's hopes of qualifying for Europe next season now rest on a top four finish in the Premiership after First Division Blackburn Rovers wrecked Gérard Houllier's FA Cup dreams. His players could boast a welter of possession but it came to nothing.'* – Paul Joyce, Liverpool Daily Post

1 Blackburn Rovers

SCORER: **Blake 84**

Sander Westerveld points towards the Blackburn goal – to encourage his strikers.

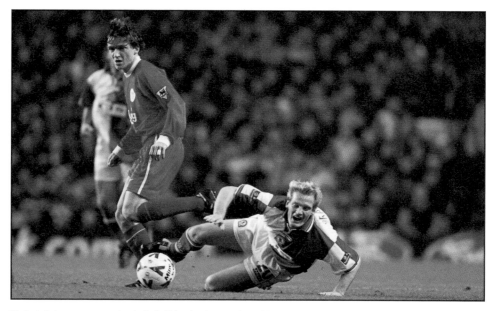

Vladimir Smicer manages to lay the ball off despite the attentions of Per Frandsen.

FILAN 1
KENNA 2
PEACOCK 5
DAILLY 23
DAVIDSON 3
JOHNSON 19
CARSLEY 6
FRANDSEN 20
DUFF 12
BLAKE 14
OSTENSTAD 10

substitutes
KELLY 13
JANSEN 15
GRAYSON 21
(for 2) 10 mins
GILLESPIE 18
(for 14) 89 mins
DUNN 27
(for 10) 76 mins

Watford 2

VENUE: Vicarage Road, 3.00pm

ATTENDANCE: 21,367

REFEREE: Stephen Lodge (Barnsley)

SCORERS: Johnson 44

Helguson 46

1 **CHAMBERLAIN**

16 **GIBBS**

4 **PAGE**

5 **PALMER**

6 **ROBINSON**

2 **LYTTLE**

35 **MILLER**

10 **JOHNSON**

26 **PERPETUINI**

37 **HELGUSON**

21 **GRAVELAINE**

substitutes

17 **SMITH**
(for 2) 83 mins

24 **BONNOT**
(for 10) 88 mins

7 **NGONGE**
(for 37) 80 mins

13 **DAY**

20 **GUDMUNDSSON**

Patrik Berger steers the ball past Chamberlain to make it 1-0.

Liverpool, single minded in their Premiership objective after the shock FA Cup exit to Blackburn, welcomed back Michael Owen and avenged their defeat by promoted Watford in their opening home game of the season – but only after losing a two-goal first half lead.

In the end Liverpool's class told but they found themselves fully extended by Graham Taylor's spirited, battling side before securing a victory that took them to fourth in the table.

Owen, given the go-ahead by a German specialist to resume playing after his hamstring trouble, returned to the attack, which meant Danny Murphy reverting to the bench. David Thompson, sent off in a reserve game the previous

Vladimir Smicer fires Liverpool's third goal – his first for the club.

3 Liverpool

SCORERS: **Berger 10**
Thompson 41
Smicer 71

Tuesday, was recalled to midfield with Steven Gerrard switched to central midfield and Jamie Carragher moving to right back.

The game was only ten minutes old when Liverpool took the lead through Patrik Berger, who extracted maximum advantage from Owen's pass after Thompson's header had caused confusion in the home defence. Liverpool doubled their lead shortly before the break when Thompson turned in Dietmar Hamann's 30-yard free kick. But with only a minute of the opening period left Watford reduced the deficit, Richard Johnson flighting a superb long range side-foot shot past Sander Westerveld after being set up by Xavier Gravelaine.

> *'I am happy because I have scored my first Liverpool goal. I have waited a long time for that moment and I hope it will be important for my confidence. But the most important thing is that we got three points.'* – Vladimir Smicer

Spectators were still taking their seas for the second half when there was another jolt for the Vicarage Road visitors within seconds of the resumption. David Perpetuini delivered a teasing free kick from the right and, as Westerveld started to advance, Watford's £1.5 million record signing Heidar Helguson found the freedom to crown his debut with a headed equaliser.

Owen threatened to put Liverpool back in front only for his run past a posse of defenders to end in a desperate goalline clearance. Liverpool's match-winner proved to be Vladimir Smicer who had been named on the bench and replaced Hamann after 63 minutes. The substitution proved inspired with the Czech firing his first Liverpool goal since his £4 million summer arrival from Lens. His low shot from the edge of the box beat Alec Chamberlain after Smicer had controlled Owen's pass from the right.

WESTERVELD 1
CARRAGHER 23
HENCHOZ 2
HYYPIA 12
MATTEO 21
THOMPSON 25
HAMANN 16
GERRARD 28
BERGER 15
OWEN 10
CAMARA 22

substitutes
NIELSEN 26
TRAORE 30
MURPHY 24
(for 10) 74 mins
SMICER 7
(for 16) 64 mins
STAUNTON 5
(for 22) 85 mins

David Thompson, scorer of Liverpool's second goal, in determined mood.

Liverpool | 0

VENUE: Anfield, 3.00pm
ATTENDANCE: 44,324
REFEREE: Steve Dunn (Bristol)

1 **WESTERVELD**
23 **CARRAGHER**
2 **HENCHOZ**
12 **HYYPIA**
21 **MATTEO**
25 **THOMPSON**
16 **HAMANN**
28 **GERRARD**
15 **BERGER**
10 **OWEN**
7 **SMICER**

substitutes

5 **STAUNTON**
26 **NIELSEN**
24 **MURPHY**
(for 25) 57 mins
18 **MEIJER**
(for 10) 28 mins
32 **NEWBY**
(for 7) 76 mins

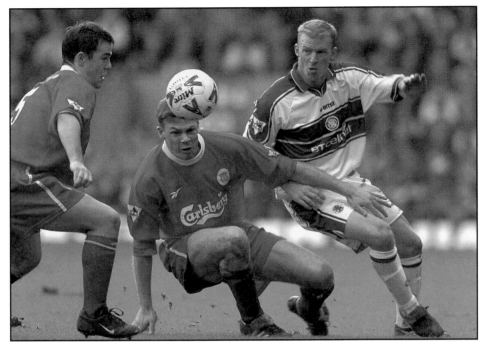

Erik Meijer and David Thompson struggle to control a bouncing ball.

A disappointing barren stalemate was further blighted for Liverpool by Michael Owen's exit in the opening half hour with renewed hamstring trouble. His departure only deepened the home side's frustration at being unable to crack embattled Boro's massed defence.

Before Owen left the action a finely judged Gary Pallister tackle denied the striker a shooting chance. Liverpool then escaped being caught out by their former captain Paul Ince, who had publicly criticised manager Gérard Houllier and his assistant Phil Thompson after his £1.25 million move to the Riverside the previous summer. Juninho's through pass put the Boro skipper clear but he hesitated looking for what seemed an inevitable offside flag. The flag was never raised but Ince's delay allowed Sander Westerveld to race out and clear the danger.

Erik Meijer's first appearance since November as Owen's replacement was soon followed by another piece of Juninho skill with a self-created opportunity. Westerveld, though, dived to his right to save the Brazilian's shot. Liverpool responded when Vladimir Smicer, operating up front in the absence of banned Titi Camara, unleashed a low effort that narrowly beat the far post. It was

0 Middlesbrough

followed by a long range Steven Gerrard effort that beat Boro keeper Mark Schwarzer but was just too high to count.

Dominic Matteo, whose pass had set up Gerrard's opportunity, set up another for Patrik Berger in the second half. But the Czech's volley was narrowly wide. And when Dietmar Hamann fired on target he was denied by Schwarzer who proceeded to produce further saves from Meijer and Gerrard. The keeper, though, was far from overworked.

> *'There was much to admire in the industry and invention of Steven Gerrard but Liverpool's problems up front, compounded by Owen's loss, were emphasised by Mark Schwarzer's relative comfort.'*
> — *Michael Calvin,* Mail on Sunday

Boro just managed to cling to their point a minute from time. Schwarzer blocked a brilliant Berger effort and substitute Danny Murphy's follow-up from the rebound was cleared off the line by Colin Cooper. The deadlock ended Liverpool's seven-game winning home Premiership run and prevented them going level with second and third placed Manchester United and Arsenal.

SCHWARZER 1
VICKERS 4
FESTA 5
PALLISTER 6
COOPER 28
FLEMING 2
SUMMERBELL 22
INCE 9
MUSTOE 7
CAMPBELL 18
JUNINHO 23

substitutes
BERESFORD 13
MADDISON 15
KILGANNON 35
GAVIN 29
(for 4) 68 mins
RICARD 19
(for 18) 82 mins

Dominic Matteo and Stephane Henchoz can only watch as Sander Westerveld takes the ball off Paul Ince's toe.

Monday 3	v	TOTTENHAM HOTSPUR	A	0-1
Monday 10	v	BLACKBURN ROVERS	H	0-1
Saturday 15	v	WATFORD	A	3-2
Saturday 22	v	MIDDLESBROUGH	H	0-0

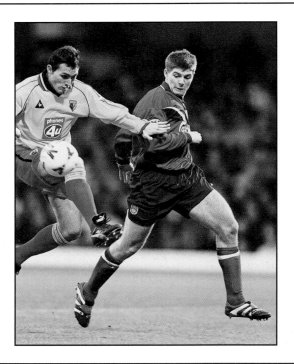

28

STEVEN GERRARD

PLAYER OF THE MONTH

A generally disappointing month for Liverpool, which produced just one win from four games, was tempered by the ever-ripening talents of Steven Gerrard. The 19-year-old local discovery had shown he was equally adept in defence or midfield, powerful in the tackle and with an ability to hit precise passes.

	P	W	D	L	F	A	Pts
Leeds United	22	15	2	5	37	25	47
Manchester United	20	13	5	2	51	2	44
Arsenal	23	13	5	5	42	23	44
LIVERPOOL	23	12	5	6	34	20	41
Sunderland	23	11	5	7	37	31	38
Chelsea	23	10	7	6	31	22	37
Tottenham Hotspur	23	10	5	8	34	27	35
West Ham United	22	8	8	6	28	25	32
Aston Villa	23	8	7	8	22	23	31
Leicester City	23	9	4	10	32	34	31
Everton	23	7	9	7	37	34	30
Coventry City	22	7	8	7	30	24	29
Wimbledon	23	6	10	7	34	37	28
Middlesbrough	21	8	4	9	24	30	28
Newcastle United	23	7	6	10	39	39	27
Derby County	23	6	5	12	23	33	23
Southampton	22	6	5	11	26	37	23
Bradford City	23	5	6	2	19	35	21
Sheffield Wednesday	22	4	4	4	20	46	16
Watford	23	4	2	17	21	50	14

UP TO AND INCLUDING MONDAY 24 JANUARY 2000

'Talking Points'

- **10/1/00 Not one of Liverpool's line-up in their last FA Cup Final** appearance in 1996 v Manchester United **played against Blackburn.** Indeed only Redknapp, Fowler and Babb were at the club in January 2000.

- **15/1/00 Liverpool's 3-2 victory at Watford was their second away win in the League** in the last eight games since the victory at Leeds on 23 August 1999.

- **22/1/00 In the last 24 games** home and away, **Liverpool have lost only three** against Boro in the League. Middlesbrough last won at Anfield in March 1976, when **Graeme Souness** and **Phil Boersma** featured in their line up.

'Talking Points'

for more info visit www.liverpoolfc.net

february

Saturday 5   v   LEEDS UNITED   H

Sunday 13   v   ARSENAL   A

Liverpool 3

VENUE: Anfield, 3.00pm

ATTENDANCE: 44,793

REFEREE: Mike Reed (Birmingham)

SCORERS: Hamann 19

Berger 69

Murphy 90

1 **WESTERVELD**

23 **CARRAGHER**

2 **HENCHOZ**

12 **HYYPIA**

21 **MATTEO**

7 **SMICER**

16 **HAMANN**

28 **GERRARD**

15 **BERGER**

22 **CAMARA**

18 **MEIJER**

substitutes

24 **MURPHY**
(for 22) 72 mins

26 **NIELSEN**

32 **NEWBY**

5 **STAUNTON**

14 **HEGGEM**

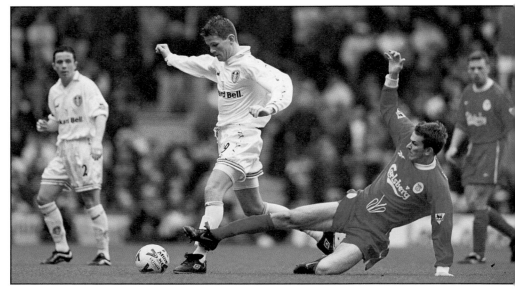

The long legs of Dietmar Hamann halt the progress of Leeds' midfielder Erik Bakke.

An exhilarating Liverpool exhibition served notice to all contenders for a Champions' League place that Gérard Houllier's team were a force to be reckoned with in the battle for a seat at Europe's top table. Despite being without injured Michael Owen, Robbie Fowler and Jamie Redknapp, banned David Thompson and Rigobert Song – who was away on African Nations Cup duty with Cameroon – Liverpool showed the strength of their squad by spectacularly shooting down their second-place foes.

Liverpool had spent a three-day break in Malta since their previous outing against Middlesbrough and an indication that their batteries were fully recharged was swiftly supplied by Patrik Berger, whose fierce shot from Dominic Matteo's pass forced Nigel Martyn into a diving save to his left to concede a corner. But Martyn was helpless when Dietmar Hamann's powerful 25-yard free kick, awarded after Vladimir Smicer had been felled, was deflected into the net off Jonathan Woodgate's left foot. It was Hamann's first Liverpool goal and the club's first at home in the new millennium.

Harry Kewell went close to putting Leeds level with a 'bender' that just beat the angle before Lee Bowyer's shot from the edge of the box was punched away by Sander Westerveld. The Yorkshire visitors finally equalised when Jason Wilcox's left wing cross from Stephen McPhail's pass was nodded in by Lee Bowyer.

1 Leeds United

SCORER: Bowyer 62

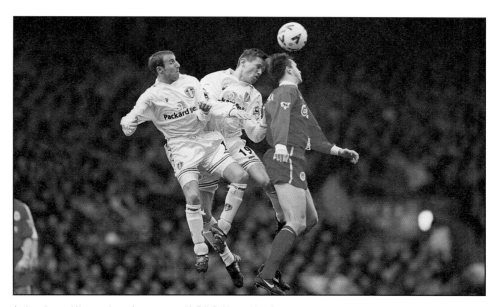

At the other end Hamann leaps for a corner with Erik Bakke and Lee Bowyer.

MARTYN 1
KELLY 2
DUBERRY 22
WOODGATE 6
HARTE 3
BOWYER 11
BAKKE 19
McPHAIL 14
WILCOX 16
KEWELL 10
SMITH 17

substitutes
HUCKERBY 12
(for 14) 76 mins
BRIDGES 8
(for 17) 76 mins
ROBINSON 13
MILLS 18
JONES 20

A stinging cross-goal volley by Erik Meijer went close to restoring Liverpool's advantage following Steven Gerrard's raking 40-yard pass from right to left. But it was Czech-mate for Leeds a few moments later when Smicer found his compatriot Berger who unleashed a 30-yard rocket that flew past Martyn. And deep into stoppage time another long range strike, this time from substitute Danny Murphy when he latched onto Michael Duberry's attempted headed clearance, arrowed into the top corner of the net.

It was a tasty end to a sweet afternoon for Gérard Houllier who had seen Liverpool lose at home by the same score to Leeds in his first match in sole charge 15 months earlier. 'We are now less naïve and more disciplined,' he observed.

This was a tremendous victory for Liverpool against one of their major rivals for a European place next season.

> *'I think Nigel Martyn is a great goalkeeper but there was nothing he could do about any of our goals. All three of them could be Goal of the Week. They were magnificent.'* – Sander Westerveld

VENUE: Highbury, 4.00pm
ATTENDANCE: 38,098
REFEREE: Steve Dunn (Bristol)

1 **SEAMAN**
2 **DIXON**
5 **KEOWN**
18 **GRIMANDI**
16 **SILVINHO**
15 **PARLOUR**
4 **VIEIRA**
17 **PETIT**
8 **LJUNGBERG**
10 **BERGKAMP**
14 **HENRY**

substitutes

11 **OVERMARS**
(for 17) 46 mins
22 **LUZHNY**
(for 8) 76 mins
9 **SUKER**
(for 10) 58 mins
13 **MANNINGER**
3 **WINTERBURN**

Liverpool impressed the watching live television gallery as they leapfrogged their Highbury opponents into third place – their highest position of the season so far – and completed their second 'double' in successive matches.

After the previous weekend's conquest of Leeds it was not surprising that Gérard Houllier paraded an unchanged side, although before the first half was complete Liverpool lost the burgeoning talent of Steven Gerrard when he limped off with groin damage. But not before he had helped clinch three crucial points which prompted Houllier to salute 'a tremendous team performance'.

Sander Westerveld made a one-handed save to deny Arsenal's spring-heeled Thierry Henry before Liverpool secured victory with a memorable 18th-minute strike by Titi Camara. The move began when the attentions of Vladimir Smicer and Jamie Carragher proved too much for Fredrik Ljungberg. When the Swede lost position Gerrard seized on the opportunity to deliver a penetrating through pass that left Arsenal's offside trap in tatters. Camara raced clear and faced with England goalkeeper David Seaman the Guinea striker and former Marseille raider calmly curled a shot into the net for his eighth goal of the season.

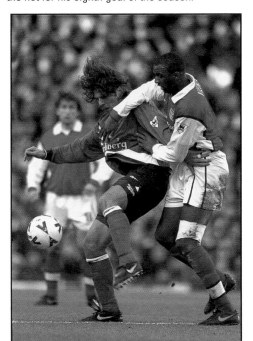

A clash of the Titans as Patriks Berger and Vieira tussle over a loose ball.

Gerrard's exit, head bowed in deep disappointment, meant Vegard Heggem going on at right back and Jamie Carragher switching to midfield.

Erik Meijer spurned a chance of doubling the lead after combining with Camara just before the interval but the Dutch striker became the second Liverpool casualty early in the second half. He over-stretched in a race for possession with Patrik Vieira which meant Danny Murphy being sent into the fray and later being denied by Seaman from an inviting opportunity.

That might have proved costly but Dominic Matteo diverted a Silvinho cross that slipped through Westerveld's grasp, with Henry heading over from the corner. Marc Overmars side-footed wide before, in a tense finish, Vieira smashed a shot against the bar.

1 Liverpool

SCORER: Camara 18

WESTERVELD 1
CARRAGHER 23
HENCHOZ 2
HYYPIA 12
MATTEO 21
SMICER 7
GERRARD 28
HAMANN 16
BERGER 15
CAMARA 22
MEIJER 18

substitutes

HEGGEM 14
(for 28) 33 mins
MURPHY 24
(for 18) 54 mins
NIELSEN 26
TRAORE 30
STAUNTON 5

'Defensively that was the best we've played since I joined the club. But we can get better. The team spirit is wonderful and the confidence high. I think everybody is giving 100 per cent on the pitch and it shows in the results we're getting. It's a very nice feeling to beat Arsenal.'
– Sami Hyypia

But Liverpool, with Sami Hyypia and Stephane Henchoz defiant at the heart of defence, held out for a notable victory to extend the club's unbeaten run against Arsenal to 14 matches.

It also offered powerful confirmation that Europe was firmly in Liverpool's sights.

Above left: Titi Camara curls the ball past David Seaman and, above right: shares the joy with the travelling Liverpool supporters.

| Saturday 5 | v | LEEDS UNITED | H | 3-1 |
| Sunday 13 | v | ARSENAL | A | 1-0 |

22

TITI CAMARA

PLAYER OF THE MONTH

Titi Camara, the player adored by the Kop, enriched his impressive contribution to Liverpool's season by scoring the only goal of the Highbury duel with Arsenal to secure a prestigious victory for Gérard Houllier's side. As a result Liverpool moved above Arsenal and into third place in the Premiership – their highest position of the season so far.

	P	W	D	L	F	A	Pts
Manchester United	26	17	6	3	59	33	57
Leeds United	26	16	3	7	39	29	51
Arsenal	26	14	5	7	46	27	47
LIVERPOOL	25	14	5	6	38	21	47
Chelsea	26	13	7	6	37	24	46
Sunderland	26	11	7	8	42	37	40
Everton	26	10	9	7	46	35	39
Aston Villa	26	10	8	8	31	24	38
Tottenham Hotspur	26	11	5	10	35	29	38
Leicester City	25	10	5	10	35	36	35
West Ham United	25	9	8	8	34	35	35
Newcastle United	26	9	7	10	46	41	34
Coventry City	26	8	8	10	35	32	32
Middlesbrough	26	9	5	12	27	37	32
Wimbledon	26	6	11	9	37	45	29
Southampton	25	8	5	12	30	41	29
Derby County	26	6	7	13	28	39	25
Bradford City	26	6	7	13	26	42	25
Sheffield Wednesday	26	4	5	17	23	53	17
Watford	26	4	3	19	23	57	15

UP TO AND INCLUDING SATURDAY 26 FEBRUARY 2000

'Talking Points'

- 5/2/00 **Liverpool completed the double** over Leeds **as they did in 1996–97** and **1997–98.**

- 5/2/00 The match against Leeds was the **50th Premiership game** played under **Gérard Houllier** and **Phil Thompson.**

- 5/2/00 In Liverpool's defeat of Leeds, **Dietmar Hamann scored his first goal for Liverpool.**

- 13/2/00 **Arsenal have not beaten Liverpool in the last 12 meetings** in the League home and away, and they have not even scored in the last six. Arsene Wenger still looks for a first win over Liverpool.

'Talking Points'

for more info visit www.liverpoolfc.net

march

Saturday 4	v	MANCHESTER UNITED	A
Saturday 11	v	SUNDERLAND	H
Wednesday 15	v	ASTON VILLA	H
Saturday 18	v	DERBY COUNTY	A
Saturday 25	v	NEWCASTLE UNITED	H

Manchester United | 1

VENUE: Old Trafford, 11.30am

ATTENDANCE: 61,592

REFEREE: Dermot Gallagher (Banbury)

SCORER: Solskjaer 45

17 **VAN DER GOUW**

2 **NEVILLE G**

6 **STAM**

27 **SILVESTRE**

3 **IRWIN**

7 **BECKHAM**

16 **KEANE**

8 **BUTT**

11 **GIGGS**

19 **YORKE**

20 **SOLSKJAER**

substitutes

1 **BOSNICH**

21 **BERG**

12 **NEVILLE P**

10 **SHERINGHAM**
(for 19) 84 mins

9 **COLE**
(for 20) 80 mins

A stirring Liverpool display against the European champions and Treble winners confirmed the rising optimism that Anfield's challenge to the might of Old Trafford was solidly based. They could even have plundered all three points from a contest in which both teams conjured winning opportunities. But it was Liverpool, who lost hamstring casualty Vegard Heggem early in the game and ankle victim Sami Hyypia for the entire second half, who emerged the happier side despite being without the banned Steven Gerrard and injured Robbie Fowler and Jamie Redknapp.

'I am pleased, delighted and very proud of my players,' proclaimed manager Gérard Houllier. 'If you want to improve you have to come to places like Old Trafford and play. That's what we did. We had some setbacks but we have now got the mental and physical strength and I would have liked to have had our full team here today.'

The clash of the northern Titans had an 11.30 morning kick off... and it was Patrik Berger who sounded the alarm call for United and the rest of the Premiership's leading pack with a stunning 27th minute free kick after Erik Meijer had been brought down by Jaap Stam. From 30 yards the Czech midfielder unleashed one of his left foot specials which flew past hapless United goalkeeper Raimond van der Gouw into the net, his shot clocked 64 mph.

> *'I had a great chance. It's hard when you come on as a sub but I would still expect to score. It was pleasing to get on, though, and hopefully I can build on that.'* – Michael Owen

Patrik Berger's free kick pierces the United wall to put Liverpool ahead.

1 Liverpool

SCORER: Berger 27

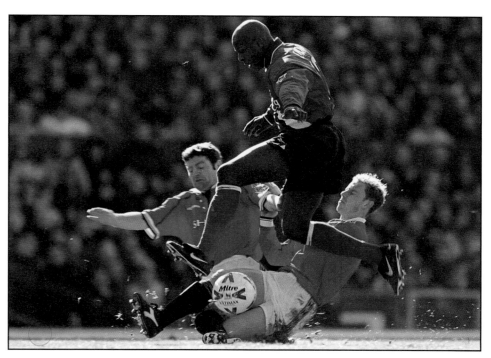

Denis Irwin and Nicky Butt combine to dispossess Titi Camara.

WESTERVELD 1
HEGGEM 14
HYYPIA 12
HENCHOZ 2
MATTEO 21
SMICER 7
CARRAGHER 23
HAMANN 16
BERGER 15
CAMARA 22
MEIJER 18

substitutes

NIELSEN 26
SONG 4
(for 14) 18 mins
STAUNTON 5
MURPHY 24
(for 12) 46 mins
OWEN 10
(for 22) 76 mins

Shortly after Berger had a chance to put Liverpool within sight of their first win at Old Trafford for a decade only for his header to be turned away by van der Gouw. Then Gary Neville rescued United by blocking a goal-bound effort from Titi Camara.

Six minutes before the interval the commanding Hyypia was hurt in a tackle by Ole Gunnar Solskjaer and went off to have five stitches in an ankle wound. Just when it seemed ten-man Liverpool would reach the break still ahead Solskjaer turned in a Ryan Giggs cross for the equaliser.

Danny Murphy replaced Hyypia for the second period in which Jamie Carragher wore the captain's armband with distinction at the heart of defence. He twice cleared off the line with Sander Westerveld beaten, first from a Giggs volley and then from United substitute Teddy Sheringham.

Liverpool, though, could point to a golden opportunity of their own just after Michael Owen's 76th-minute entrance as a substitute following his latest hamstring absence. Owen raced onto Murphy's superb through pass with only van der Gouw to beat… but his shot curled agonisingly wide of the far post with the keeper beaten.

Liverpool | 1

VENUE: Anfield, 3.00pm
ATTENDANCE: 44,693
REFEREE: Graham Poll (Tring)

SCORER: Berger 2 (penalty)

1 **WESTERVELD**
21 **MATTEO**
12 **HYYPIA**
2 **HENCHOZ**
4 **SONG**
15 **BERGER**
16 **HAMANN**
23 **CARRAGHER**
28 **GERRARD**
18 **MEIJER**
8 **HESKEY**

substitutes
5 **STAUNTON**
19 **FRIEDEL**
22 **CAMARA**
(for 4) 82 mins
24 **MURPHY**
(for 28) 46 mins
10 **OWEN**
(for 18) 76 mins

New signing Emile Heskey did not take long to make his presence felt in a Liverpool shirt.

A packed, sun-splashed Anfield welcomed new £11 million record signing Emile Heskey as the England raider plunged into his Liverpool debut the day after his big move from Leicester.

Heskey's arrival squeezed Titi Camara onto the bench and it took the costly recruit less than three minutes to make a major impact for his new club when his surge down the right flank and run into the box from a Rigobert Song pass was ended when he was brought down by Darren Williams. Referee Graham Poll signalled a penalty and Patrik Berger blasted the spot kick past Thomas Sorensen for his eighth goal of the season on his 100th Premiership appearance for Liverpool.

Yet somehow Liverpool lost their edge after that early breakthrough and Sunderland appealed for a penalty of their own when Niall Quinn claimed he had been impeded by Stephane Henchoz. Referee Poll, though, was unmoved.

Too many Liverpool scoring attempts were off target but when Dietmar Hamann unleashed an accurate long range 'dipper' Sorensen tipped his shot over the bar. The visiting keeper also kept out a second half header from Erik Meijer with his counterpart Sander Westerveld doing likewise from a Kevin Phillips header.

| 1 | **Sunderland** |

SCORER: Phillips 77 (penalty)

Steven Gerrard, back in the side after a groin injury and suspension in place of ankle casualty Vladimir Smicer, made way in the second half for Danny Murphy who, together with Meijer, did put the ball in the net but both were offside. Liverpool just could not increase their advantage, despite the power and pace of Heskey, Michael Owen's introduction in place of Meijer and the late entrance of Camara in place of Song.

Their slender lead was finally wiped out 12 minutes from the end when Phillips, pursuing a

> *'We knew it would be a hard game but I thought I did reasonably well. I did feel nervous. But once the game began and I got my first touch I was all right.'* – Emile Heskey

chance created by Quinn, was brought down out on the right of the penalty area by Westerveld. This time referee Poll did point to the spot and Phillips lashed his kick into the roof of the Kop net.

An afternoon that had promised so much for Liverpool ended in frustration and disappointment.

SORENSEN 1
MAKIN 2
WILLIAMS 18
CRADDOCK 17
HOLLOWAY 14
KILBANE 4
SCHWARZ 20
RAE 16
THIRLWELL 19
PHILLIPS 10
QUINN 9

substitutes
BUTLER 6
SUMMERBEE 7
MARRIOTT 13
ROY 29
REDDY 31

Power and pace – two of Heskey's key qualities – were shown in abundance during his first match for his new club.

Liverpool | 0

VENUE: Anfield, 7.45pm
ATTENDANCE: 43,615
REFEREE: Steve Bennett (Orpington)

1 **WESTERVELD**
23 **CARRAGHER**
12 **HYYPIA**
2 **HENCHOZ**
21 **MATTEO**
25 **THOMPSON**
28 **GERRARD**
16 **HAMANN**
15 **BERGER**
10 **OWEN**
8 **HESKEY**

substitutes

19 **FRIEDEL**
5 **STAUNTON**
18 **MEIJER**
(for 25) 83 mins
11 **REDKNAPP**
(for 28) 78 mins
22 **CAMARA**
(for 10) 67 mins

Villa's visit brought Michael Owen's return to Liverpool's starting line-up for the first time in five games spanning two months. But for the second successive home match they were pegged to a draw, although it was sufficient to lift them into third place.

It was not a happy night for Owen who missed a penalty awarded for visiting captain Gareth Southgate's foul on Patrik Berger with just over half an hour gone.

With Berger still dusting himself down from Southgate's challenge Owen put the ball on the spot and blasted the penalty onto the underside of Peter Enckelman's bar. When it bounced down the referee's assistant ruled that the ball had not crossed the line.

In the opening minutes Emile Heskey had delivered one of his menacing trademark crosses which evaded the recalled David Thompson.

Prior to the penalty Owen had seen his shot from Steven Gerrard's sublime pass saved by Enckelman's legs just after Villa had gone even closer to breaking the deadlock. Julian Joachim seemed certain to score when his shot beat Sander Westerveld but it was cleared off the line by Stephane Henchoz.

In the second half Owen fired over the bar and Thompson tested Enckelman with

Titi Camara's pace worried the Villa defenders, but the second-half substitute failed to find the back of the net.

0   **Aston Villa**

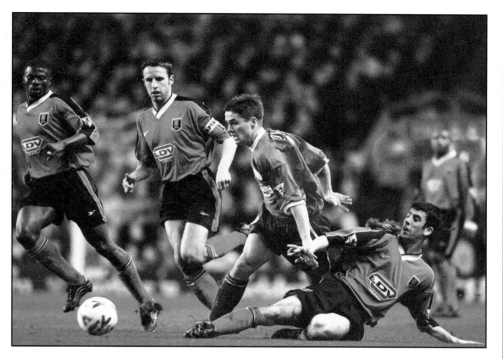

Back from injury, Michael Owen had a frustrating game that included a missed penalty.

ENCKELMAN 39
SOUTHGATE 4
EHIOGU 5
BARRY 15
DELANEY 24
BOATENG 6
MERSON 10
STONE 26
WRIGHT 3
CARBONE 18
JOACHIM 12

substitutes
WATSON 2
CUTLER 13
TAYLOR 7
(for 4) 53 mins
HENDRIE 17
(for 10) 61 mins
WALKER 19
(for 12) 89 mins

a shot saved by the keeper before Villa again went close as Ian Taylor's header just beat the post. Benito Carbone and Steve Stone combined in another Villa raid which ended with Stone flighting his cross just behind substitute Lee Hendrie.

Liverpool sent on Titi Camara for Owen, gave Jamie Redknapp his first senior action since November as a late replacement for Gerrard and withdrew Thompson in favour of Erik Meijer. But the changes failed to produce a goal and the result meant that Liverpool had not scored from open play for three games.

> *'Liverpool achieved one goal, moving into the cherished Champions'*
> *League places, but they could not get one where it mattered. For the*
> *second time in four days they were the dominant force at Anfield but*
> *were reined back to a point.'* – Guy Hodgson, *The* Independent

Derby County | 0

VENUE: Pride Park 3.00pm

ATTENDANCE: 33,378

REFEREE: Barry Knight (Orpington)

21 **POOM**

19 **ELLIOTT**

2 **CARBONARI**

16 **LAURSEN**

10 **DELAP**

29 **ERANIO**

4 **POWELL**

27 **KINKLADZE**

7 **JOHNSON**

35 **STRUPAR**

12 **CHRISTIE**

substitutes

24 **OAKES**

17 **PRIOR**

26 **ROBINSON**

3 **SCHNOOR**
(for 2) 78 mins

8 **STURRIDGE**
(for 4) 84 mins

Liverpool extracted maximum revenge for being victims of a Derby double the previous season – their first over the Anfield side for almost 30 years – by completing their own double over the Pride Park club to stay third in the Premiership.

Manager Gérard Houllier was able to take the rare decision of naming an unchanged side which broke the deadlock in superb style after Georgiou Kinkladze had fired wide for Derby and Malcolm Christie had failed to connect with a Rory Delap header from a Kinkladze cross.

With 17 minutes on the clock the imposing Sami Hyypia broke up a home attack, took one glance and delivered a raking 40-yard pass into the path of Michael Owen on the right edge of the Derby penalty area.

The England striker sidestepped Jacob Laursen before driving a shot across Derby keeper Mart Poom for his ninth goal of the season and his first of the new millennium.

It was a move wonderfully created and executed in front of a 33,000-plus record crowd at Derby's new stadium. Owen threatened again shortly before the interval when he latched onto Emile Heskey's flick from Sander Westerveld's goal kick. But this time his shot was well saved by Poom.

Derby's attempts to haul themselves back into the contest gave adventurous Liverpool even more attacking scope. But Steven Gerrard fired over after a Heskey cross was deflected and when Patrik Berger put Owen in his shot went wide.

Jamie Carragher had a tireless game in defence.

Branko Strupar's header straight to Westerveld reminded Liverpool of the fragility of their lead and it was not until six minutes from the end that they secured the points when Owen's

2 Liverpool

SCORERS: Owen 17

Camara 84

replacement Titi Camara strode onto Dominic Matteo's pass, went past Steve Elliott and despatched his ninth goal of the season past Poom.

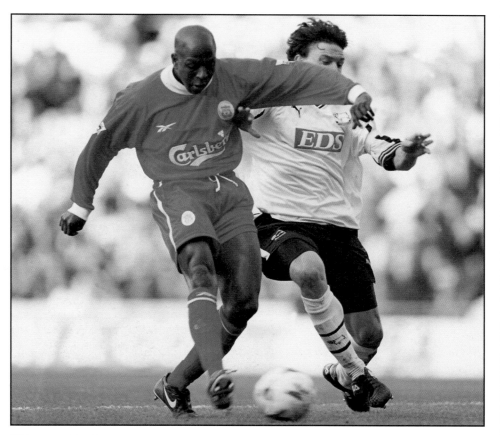

Titi Camara put himself on the scoresheet with his ninth goal of the season.

WESTERVELD 1
CARRAGHER 23
HYYPIA 12
HENCHOZ 2
MATTEO 21
THOMPSON 25
GERRARD 28
HAMANN 16
BERGER 15
OWEN 10
HESKEY 8

substitutes

CAMARA 22
(for 10) 71 mins
REDKNAPP 11
(for 8) 87 mins
FRIEDEL 19
STAUNTON 5
MEIJER 18

'It was great to score and it's a big psychological boost. It seems a long time since my last goal and after missing the penalty against Villa in midweek it was good to give something back to the lads. But I've got some strengthening and sharpening work to do before I'm back to my best.' – Michael Owen

Liverpool 2

VENUE: Anfield, 3.00pm

ATTENDANCE: 44,743

REFEREE: Paul Durkin (Portland)

SCORERS: Camara 51

Redknapp 88

1 **WESTERVELD**

23 **CARRAGHER**

2 **HENCHOZ**

12 **HYYPIA**

21 **MATTEO**

25 **THOMPSON**

28 **GERRARD**

16 **HAMANN**

15 **BERGER**

22 **CAMARA**

8 **HESKEY**

substitutes

18 **MEIJER**
(for 25) 76 mins

11 **REDKNAPP**
(for 28) 78 mins

24 **MURPHY**
(for 15) 87 mins

4 **SONG**

19 **FRIEDEL**

A late header from comeback captain Jamie Redknapp clinched a crucial victory for Liverpool and crowned an inspired substitution by manager Gérard Houllier.

With the game deadlocked at 1-1, only three minutes left on the clock and Bobby Robson's visitors seemingly destined for a share of the spoils Redknapp rose to meet Danny Murphy's corner and head the winner beyond Shay Given, beating Warren Barton's desperate attempts to keep it out of the net.

It was club skipper Redknapp's third substitute appearance after a four-month absence following knee surgery. But the significance of his third goal of his injury-ravaged season was heightened by Europe-qualifying rivals Chelsea being held to a home draw by Southampton the same afternoon and Leeds losing at Leicester the next day.

The story of the match also vindicated Houllier's decision to rest Michael Owen and recall Titi Camara. The Guinea striker responded by firing Liverpool ahead early in the second half.

The reds had the ball in the net a mere 11 seconds into the match through David Thompson, but referee Paul Durkin ruled it out for the Birkenhead-born midfielder's push on Steve Howey.

It took Liverpool until midway through the first half to mount another shot on target, Shay Given saving Emile Heskey's angled attempt. The Newcastle goalkeeper did likewise from a Dietmar Hamann free-kick while Nikos Dabizas made a crucial interception from Steve Gerrard after a slip from Howey let in the Liverpool teenager.

Although Liverpool's defence were keeping a tight rein on Newcastle's much-vaunted strike force of Alan Shearer and Duncan Ferguson their own scoring chances were rationed.

Emile Heskey and Kieron Dyer, England team-mates, demonstrate their willingness to win.

1 | Newcastle United

SCORER: Shearer 67

Jamie Redknapp's appearance as a substitute was crowned when this header crashed into the Newcastle net two minutes from time.

GIVEN 1
GOMA 5
HOWEY 6
DABIZAS 34
BARTON 2
DYER 7
LEE 37
SPEED 11
HUGHES 18
SHEARER 9
FERGUSON 20

substitutes
HARPER 13
KETSBAIA 14
ANTUNES 38
DOMI 4
(for 5) 57 mins
GALLACHER 32
(for 37) 66 mins

There was an explosion of relief as well as celebration when Camara smashed the deadlock as he connected at the far post with Gerrard's cross from the right. It was the Guinea striker's tenth goal of the season. It was cancelled out 16 minutes later by Shearer, who managed at last to elude his markers and head an Aaron Hughes cross past Sander Westerveld. With time ticking away Houllier sent on Redknapp in place of Gerrard, a decision fate rewarded when the substitute scored the match winner.

> *'That's the most important goal I've scored because we all want to be playing Champions' League football next season. I've scored only once before with a header and that was for England Under 21s. So this was a very emotional moment for me. It's been a long four months out but that goal has made the wait and all the effort worthwhile.'* – Jamie Redknapp

Saturday 4	v	MANCHESTER UNITED	A	1-1
Saturday 11	v	SUNDERLAND	H	1-1
Wednesday 15	v	ASTON VILLA	H	0-0
Saturday 18	v	DERBY COUNTY	A	2-0
Saturday 25	v	NEWCASTLE UNITED	H	2-1

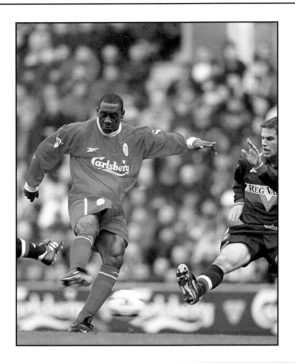

8

EMILE HESKEY

PLAYER OF THE MONTH

Emile Heskey arrived as Liverpool's £11 million record signing and swiftly made an impact with his powerful surges at opposing defences and his menacing crosses from either flank. Gérard Houllier's injection of Heskey's talents into the Liverpool squad clearly increased its attacking potency.

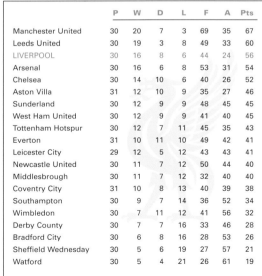

	P	W	D	L	F	A	Pts
Manchester United	30	20	7	3	69	35	67
Leeds United	30	19	3	8	49	33	60
LIVERPOOL	30	16	8	6	44	24	56
Arsenal	30	16	6	8	53	31	54
Chelsea	30	14	10	6	40	26	52
Aston Villa	31	12	10	9	35	27	46
Sunderland	30	12	9	9	48	45	45
West Ham United	30	12	9	9	41	40	45
Tottenham Hotspur	30	12	7	11	45	35	43
Everton	31	10	11	10	49	42	41
Leicester City	29	12	5	12	43	43	41
Newcastle United	30	11	7	12	50	44	40
Middlesbrough	30	11	7	12	32	40	40
Coventry City	31	10	8	13	40	39	38
Southampton	30	9	7	14	36	52	34
Wimbledon	30	7	11	12	41	56	32
Derby County	30	7	7	16	33	46	28
Bradford City	30	6	8	16	28	53	26
Sheffield Wednesday	30	5	6	19	27	57	21
Watford	30	5	4	21	26	61	19

UP TO AND INCLUDING SUNDAY 26 MARCH 2000

'Talking Points'

- 4/3/00 **Liverpool's last win** at Old Trafford came in **March 1990.**

- 4/3/00 In the last ten visits to Old Trafford, **Liverpool have drawn six and lost four.**

- 11/3/00 **Sunderland have only managed two League wins on their visits to Anfield since 1936 in the League, and scored only five times in the last ten visits.**

- 18/3/00 **Michael Owen scored his first goal since 28 December** against Wimbledon.

- 18/3/00 **Liverpool did the double over Derby**, to avenge County's feat against Liverpool last season.

'Talking Points'

for more info visit www.liverpoolfc.net

april

Saturday 1	v	COVENTRY CITY	A
Sunday 9	v	TOTTENHAM HOTSPUR	H
Sunday 16	v	WIMBLEDON	A
Friday 21	v	EVERTON	A
Saturday 29	v	CHELSEA	A

Coventry City 0

VENUE: **Highfield Road, 3.00pm**
ATTENDANCE: **23,098**
REFEREE: **Mike Reed (Birmingham)**

26 **OGRIZOVIC**
12 **TELFER**
5 **SHAW**
35 **HENDRY**
16 **FROGGATT**
18 **CHIPPO**
10 **MCALLISTER**
24 **EUSTACE**
11 **HADJI**
8 **WHELAN**
31 **ROUSSEL**

substitutes

17 **BREEN**
3 **BURROWS**
33 **KIRKLAND**
22 **QUINN**
(for 24) 66 mins
7 **KEANE**
(for 8) 33 mins

Richard Shaw, along with most of the Coventry City defence, found Michael Owen too hot to handle.

A superb scoring brace from recalled Michael Owen and Emile Heskey's first goal for his new club secured an emphatic Liverpool triumph which lifted them to within a point of second-placed Leeds United, who lost at home to Chelsea.

It was April Fool's Day but there was no fooling around from Gérard Houllier's side. Their victory could have been massive but for the heroics of former Liverpool goalkeeper Steve Ogrizovic on his 600th appearance for Coventry. 'Oggy', at 42 and a half, produced stunning saves from Owen, Heskey and David Thompson to prevent Liverpool's winning margin reaching embarrassing proportions for the home side.

But even he was powerless to deny Owen on the England striker's return to action after being rested for the previous game against Newcastle. Midway through the first half Owen seized on a Dominic Matteo pass on the edge of the box. He rounded Richard Shaw and Colin Hendry before unleashing a shot out of Ogrizovic's reach for a goal of sheer brilliance.

Before the first half was out Owen had struck again and once more he was set up by Matteo. Heskey launched the move on the left and linked with Steven Gerrard. The teenage midfielder's

3   Liverpool

SCORERS: Owen 23, 38
                Heskey 78

pass found the overlapping Matteo whose cross allowed Owen to strike with unerring accuracy at the far post. Liverpool – stripped of previous match winner Redknapp's presence in the squad after he sustained an ankle injury in the reserves – went close through a Gerrard shot that went over and a Thompson blast brilliantly saved by the age-mocking Ogrizovic.

Coventry responded with a powerful effort from Mustapha Hadji that just beat Sander Westerveld's woodwork but his counterpart Ogrizovic impressed again, this time denying Owen a hat-trick by saving with his legs.

But Liverpool did apply a fair gloss to the scoreline when Heskey capped another fine individual performance with his first Liverpool goal, a towering header from Patrik Berger's free-kick.

> *'Michael Owen is a tremendous finisher and looked extremely sharp and I was delighted Emile Heskey got his first goal for us. He's a great player because he's a team player. In every goal, every movement he's involved. Above that, his gelling with the team has been fantastic.'*
>
> *– Gérard Houllier*

WESTERVELD 1
CARRAGHER 23
HENCHOZ 2
HYYPIA 12
MATTEO 21
THOMPSON 25
HAMANN 16
GERRARD 28
BERGER 15
OWEN 10
HESKEY 8

substitutes
FRIEDEL 19
MEIJER 18
SONG 4
(for 2) 85 mins
MURPHY 14
(for 28) 69 mins
CAMARA 22
(for 10) 79 mins

New Order: Emile Heskey outpaces Gary McAllister, on the way to scoring his first Liverpool goal.

Liverpool 2

VENUE: **Anfield, 3.00pm**
ATTENDANCE: **44,536**
REFEREE: **Stephen Lodge (Barnsley)**

SCORERS: **Berger 34**
Owen 61

1 **WESTERVELD**
23 **CARRAGHER**
2 **HENCHOZ**
12 **HYYPIA**
21 **MATTEO**
25 **THOMPSON**
24 **MURPHY**
16 **HAMANN**
15 **BERGER**
10 **OWEN**
8 **HESKEY**

substitutes

7 **SMICER**
(for 25) 73 mins
14 **HEGGEM**
(for 24) 84 mins
22 **CAMARA**
(for 10) 88 mins
26 **NIELSEN**
4 **SONG**

A magnificent trademark strike by Patrik Berger put Liverpool on course for a victory that sent them leapfrogging Leeds United into second place in the Premiership – their highest position for 19 months.

'This is a very important day for us,' enthused manager Gérard Houllier, who this time rested Steven Gerrard and brought in Danny Murphy. 'It's the best position we've been in for a long time and it's a kind of reward for the players.

'From our ninth League fixture against Aston Villa in October we've taken 52 points which competes with Manchester United's performance and shows the progress of our team.'

> *'Emile and I have played together through a few different age groups for England and the manager here has been encouraging us to work off each other. He's a great player. He's always looking to bring others into the game and he presents problems to every defence.'* – Michael Owen

Michael Owen's 61st minute goal sealed the win for Liverpool, although Tottenham created few chances.

0 Tottenham Hotspur

Emile Heskey was closely guarded all afternoon by the Tottenham defence.

WALKER 1
CARR 2
CAMPBELL 5
PERRY 6
TARICCO 3
IVERSEN 10
ANDERTON 7
FREUND 4
CLEMENCE 25
GINOLA 14
ARMSTRONG 16

substitutes
BAARDSEN 13
KORSTEN 11
YOUNG 21
DAVIES 29
(for 25) 80 mins
ETHERINGTON 28
(for 14) 80 mins

A Tottenham side sent out by their manager George Graham with the task of nullifying Liverpool's attacking threat must have fancied their chances of reaching half time unscathed when Berger literally smashed the deadlock ten minutes before the interval.

Even when David Thompson carried on a move started by Dietmar Hamann there did not seem much scope for Berger. But the Czech Republic star wheeled around and cracked a stupendous 25-yard shot that had the ball bulging the Kop net for his ninth goal of the season before Ian Walker even had the chance to see it.

The Tottenham goalkeeper was equally powerless to intervene shortly before the break when Heskey eluded Sol Campbell and his fellow defenders to let fly with a blistering left-foot shot that almost cracked the bar.

Berger turned provider in the second half to twice set up David Thompson, first for a shot saved by Walker and then for the midfielder to find himself one-on-one with the keeper only to have the ball snatched from his feet.

Negative Tottenham's rigid reliance on trying to deny Liverpool space was bound to backfire on them again and it did with just over an hour of the match gone.

When the constantly-threatening Heskey saw his shot saved by Walker he crossed the ball back to Michael Owen to wrap up the points. The goal was a reward for the developing interplay between Owen and Heskey and extended Liverpool's Premiership sequence to just two defeats in 24 outings, their move into second place being their highest position since September 1998.

Wimbledon 1

VENUE: Selhurst Park 1.15pm
ATTENDANCE: 26,102
REFEREE: Mike Riley (Leeds)

SCORER: Andresen 70

1 **SULLIVAN**

21 **JUPP**

5 **BLACKWELL**

30 **HREIDARSSON**

2 **CUNNINGHAM**

7 **CORT**

29 **ANDERSEN**

4 **ROBERTS**

16 **HUGHES**

32 **LUND**

11 **GAYLE**

substitutes

13 **HEALD**

19 **BADIR**

24 **FRANCIS**

15 **LEABURN**
(for 5) 86 mins

20 **ANDRESEN**
(for 32) 58 mins

Liverpool players wore black armbands on the weekend of the 11th anniversary of the Hillsborough Disaster and a minute's silence was impeccably observed by the 26,000-plus Selhurst Park crowd prior to the 1.15pm kick-off . And when the dust had settled after the action on the pitch – which took Liverpool five points clear of third-placed Arsenal – manager Gérard Houllier's first public response was to remember the Hillsborough victims and their families.

Heskey's second and third Liverpool goals came in this game against relegation-bound Wimbledon.

'I think the players and myself were very conscious of what winning today means,' he said. 'We dedicate it to the fans and to the families who suffered at Hillsborough. It is a special day and nowhere was the minute's silence more emotional than here at our game.'

The victory was Liverpool's first in nine visits to Wimbledon and provided another pay-back by Emile Heskey for Houllier's faith and £11 million investment in the England raider's talents.

Two goals by the former Leicester star gave Liverpool three precious points in their bid for automatic Champions' League qualification on a day when Steven Gerrard, rested for the previous

2 Liverpool

SCORER: Heskey 36, 64

Michael Hughes and Michael Owen tussle for possession with the Liverpool striker coming out on top.

WESTERVELD 1
CARRAGHER 23
HENCHOZ 2
HYYPIA 12
MATTEO 21
THOMPSON 25
HAMANN 16
GERRARD 28
BERGER 15
OWEN 10
HESKEY 8

substitutes

SMICER 7
(for 25) 62 mins

MURPHY 24
(for 10) 82 mins

CAMARA 22
(for 8) 77 mins

HEGGEM 14

NIELSEN 26

game, returned to midfield, with Danny Murphy reverting to the bench.

Heskey might have broken the deadlock after only 11 minutes when he was set up by a superb Dietmar Hamann pass. His shot, though, hit onrushing home goalkeeper Neil Sullivan. Hamann himself had also forced Sullivan into a fingertip save to extend the barren scoreline.

But Heskey made no mistake nine minutes before the interval when he applied an emphatic finish to a Michael Owen pass. Wimbledon, whose five straight defeats going into their collision with Liverpoool left them dangling just above the relegation abyss, summoned up more resolve after the interval.

Dominic Matteo made a timely intervention to deny Andreas Lund a shot while Sander Westerveld kept out a Michael Hughes effort before Heskey struck again, rising high above the home defence to head in Patrik Berger's 64th-minute corner.

Berger should have made it 3-0 but failed to accept a clear chance created by substitute Vladimir Smicer and Owen. Wimbledon proceeded to cut the deficit to a single goal when substitute Martin Andresen headed past Westerveld following a corner conceded by the Liverpool goalkeeper's save off Hermann Hreidarsson's close-range volley.

But Liverpool's twin central defensive pillars Sami Hyypia and Stephane Henchoz smashed home hopes of an equaliser and the only negative note for the visitors was Heskey's 77th-minute exit with a back injury.

> *'Emile's contribution to the result was outstanding. There was a lot of scepticism when he was brought in but we know what he contributes and what he brings to us. This is the first time Liverpool have won here in ten years. We are in the final straight and we have to keep going.'*
> – *Gérard Houllier*

Everton 0

VENUE: Goodison Park 8.00pm

ATTENDANCE: 40,052

REFEREE: Graham Poll (Tring)

13 **GERRARD**

15 **DUNNE**

19 **XAVIER**

14 **WEIR**

6 **UNSWORTH**

12 **PEMBRIDGE**

7 **COLLINS**

18 **HUGHES S.**

8 **BARMBY**

10 **HUTCHISON**

26 **HUGHES M.**

substitutes

3 **BALL**
(for 12) 84 mins

21 **WARD**
(for 8) 88 mins

17 **JEFFERS**
(for 26) 81 mins

20 **JEVONS**

35 **SIMONSEN**

The 162nd League meeting of these old adversaries failed to produce a goal but did engineer drama and controversy in the grand tradition of Mersey derbies, which now span three separate centuries.

This seventh meeting of the clubs on a Good Friday was their first collision of the new millennium and the tension was evident from the outset as the teams pursued points to bolster their respective European qualifying ambitions.

Unchanged Liverpool, without international absentees Rigobert

Heskey rides an Everton challenge prior to his half time withdrawl.

Song and Titi Camara but with Robbie Fowler back in the 16 for the first time in 15 games covering more than three months, had the first clear scoring chance early in the contest.

But Michael Owen, challenged by David Unsworth, saw his shot saved by Paul Gerrard. The Everton goalkeeper again thwarted the England striker from a David Thompson cross after a powerful run by Emile Heskey, whose back injury from a heavy fall forced his half-time withdrawal and meant Fowler's eagerly awaited senior return.

Perhaps Owen realised his luck was out when he linked with Steven Gerrard soon after the interval only for Everton's Gerrard to make a fingertip save and deny him for a third time .

Liverpool, though, had their hearts in their mouths when a John Collins pass allowed Mark Pembridge to steer the ball into the path of Mark Hughes, so often in the past the Anfield club's tormentor.

This time though, the Wales striker's shot beat Sander Westerveld but also flashed wide of the far post. The Dutch keeper proceeded to save at the foot of the post from Pembridge while at the other end Gerrard parried a Patrik Berger blast before Liverpool substitute Vegard Heggem saw his point-blank shot held by the Everton keeper.

Then came the bizarre climax.

With only seconds remaining of two announced minutes of stoppage time Liverpool goalkeeper Sander Westerveld's quickly taken free-kick struck Everton's Don Hutchison – a former Liverpool player – on the back as he was walking away and rebounded into the net.

0 Liverpool

But the 'goal' did not stand, referee Graham Poll explaining: 'I looked at my watch and I thought as he (Westerveld) kicked it out 'its the last kick of the game – it's finished.' The ball hit the player (Hutchison) who wasn't anywhere near ten yards away so the issue is largely irrelevant .

'The referee is the sole arbiter of time. My time was up, we'd added on the correct amount of time for stoppages. The players got a bit excited and confused as they do in derby matches. But I was clear in my mind.'

'We came here to win. We wanted the three points. We're playing for the Champions' League so we're not really happy with a draw. But we're still second in the League and all through the season everybody has been really positive.' – Sander Westerveld

WESTERVELD 1
CARRAGHER 23
HENCHOZ 2
HYYPIA 12
MATTEO 21
THOMPSON 25
GERRARD 28
HAMANN 16
BERGER 15
OWEN 10
HESKEY 8

substitutes
SMICER 7
MURPHY 24
NIELSEN 26
HEGGEM 14
(for 25) 56 mins
FOWLER 9
(for 8) 45 mins

Stephan Henchoz – in the heat of the Mersey derby – battles with Everton's Welsh veteran Mark Hughes.

Chelsea | 2

VENUE: Stamford Bridge, 3.00pm

ATTENDANCE: 34,957

REFEREE: Graham Barber (Kingston)

SCORERS: Weah 2
Di Matteo 14

1 **DE GOEY**

15 **MELCHIOT**

6 **DESAILLY**

5 **LEBOEUF**

3 **BABAYARO**

16 **DI MATTEO**

20 **MORRIS**

11 **WISE**

34 **HARLEY**

31 **WEAH**

25 **ZOLA**

substitutes

23 **CUDICINI**

18 **AMBROSETTI**

8 **POYET**
(for 3) 45 mins

30 **THOME**
(for 20) 69 mins

9 **SUTTON**
(for 31) 80 mins

A below par performance from Liverpool ended with their 13-game unbeaten Premiership run being brought to a halt by a Chelsea side who recaptured their cutting edge after a public blast from manager Gianluca Vialli.

First-half goals from George Weah and Roberto Di Matteo secured victory for the London club and meant that Liverpool lost ground in the scramble for Champions' League places.

Arsenal, who won 1-0 at Everton while Liverpool were losing at Stamford Bridge, leapfrogged Gérard Houllier's side into second place and increased their goal difference advantage on their Merseyside rivals to six. The following day Leeds won at Sheffield Wednesday to move fourth, just two points behind.

Vladimir Smicer's illness ruled him out of a comeback and the Liverpool manager recalled Danny Murphy in place of David Thompson, who was omitted even from a place on the bench.

Just a point from the game would have been sufficient to guarantee Liverpool European football in the UEFA Cup. But their ambitions were swiftly rocked on a ground where they have yet to win in the Premiership. They have now made ten League visits since their last success in December 1989, en route

Take off: Emile Heskey and Marcel Desailly compete for aerial dominance.

0 Liverpool

to the championship.

There were less than two minutes on the clock when Mario Melchiot linked with Di Matteo. The Italian international exposed a huge hole in the Liverpool defence to supply Weah and the Liberian

> **'This was not the true face of Liverpool FC today. We were sloppy at the back, got punished and we had only half chances. I had begun to wonder why we looked so poor and then I realised it was because Chelsea were playing so superbly. But we didn't show the best of ourselves and we have to be careful in the final straight.'** – *Gérard Houllier*

dispatched a precise shot into the far corner of the net as Sander Westerveld advanced.

Weah would have scored again shortly after if it had not been for the alertness of Westerveld. The Dutch goalkeeper dashed off his line to win a race with the African to reach Celestine Babayaro's probing pass and clear the danger.

But Weah, former World Footballer of the Year, turned creator for Chelsea to double their advantage in the 14th minute.

Dennis Wise played the ball forward for Weah to exchange passes with Gianfranco Zola and provide Di Matteo with an invitation he clinically accepted.

Referee Graham Barber rejected three Liverpool penalty claims: for Ed De Goey's challenge on Patrik Berger, for handling by Di Matteo and for a Marcel Desailly tackle on Emile Heskey. But although Liverpool improved in the second half, when Robbie Fowler, Jamie Redknapp and Titi Camara went on as substitutes, Chelsea were worthy winners on a day when Heskey and Owen were starved of chances.

Steven Gerrard goes flat out on a Stamford Bridge stage that has not been kind to Liverpool for a long time.

WESTERVELD 1
CARRAGHER 23
HENCHOZ 2
HYYPIA 12
MATTEO 21
MURPHY 24
GERRARD 28
HAMANN 16
BERGER 15
HESKEY 8
OWEN 10

substitutes
FOWLER 9
(for 24) 75 mins
REDKNAPP 11
(for 28) 50 mins
CAMARA 22
(for 15) 60 mins
SONG 4
NIELSEN 26

Saturday 1	v	COVENTRY CITY	A	3-0
Sunday 9	v	TOTTENHAM HOTSPUR	H	2-0
Sunday 16	v	WIMBLEDON	A	2-1
Friday 21	v	EVERTON	A	0-0
Saturday 29	v	CHELSEA	A	0-2

21

DOMINIC MATTEO

PLAYER OF THE MONTH

Dominic Matteo, whose Anfield future was queried by many pundits earlier in the season, responded with a series of fine displays to repay the belief in his talents shown by Gérard Houllier and his backroom staff and make the left back berth his own. 'We had faith in Dominic and we are getting the rewards of that,' said Houllier. 'He's very professional, very focused and works hard.'

	P	W	D	L	F	A	Pts
Manchester United	35	25	7	3	90	42	82
LIVERPOOL	34	19	9	6	51	25	66
Arsenal	33	19	6	8	63	34	63
Leeds United	34	19	4	11	51	41	61
Chelsea	35	16	11	8	46	32	59
Aston Villa	35	15	11	9	43	31	56
Sunderland	35	15	9	11	54	52	54
West Ham United	34	15	9	10	51	49	54
Everton	35	12	13	10	58	45	49
Tottenham Hotspur	35	14	7	14	52	44	49
Leicester City	34	13	7	14	48	50	46
Newcastle United	34	12	8	14	55	50	44
Middlesbrough	34	12	8	14	40	49	44
Coventry City	35	11	8	16	43	50	41
Southampton	35	11	7	17	42	60	40
Derby County	35	9	9	17	43	52	36
Wimbledon	35	7	11	17	44	67	32
Bradford City	35	7	9	19	34	65	30
Sheffield Wednesday	34	7	6	21	30	60	27
Watford	34	5	5	24	30	70	20

UP TO AND INCLUDING MONDAY 24 APRIL 2000

'Talking Points'

- 9/4/00 **Tottenham's dismal record at Anfield continued** – since 1911 they've won only three times there in the League.

- 21/4/00 **Liverpool won their fifth successive game of the season** against Wimbledon who lost for the sixth successive time, to plunge them closer to relegation.

- 21/4/00 **Liverpool** have **won only once** in the last 12 meetings against Everton, and **have not won at Goodison in the last nine visits.**

- 29/4/00 **Liverpool have yet to win at Chelsea** in the Premiership and have won only twice in the last 17 visits.

'Talking Points'

for more info visit www.liverpoolfc.net

may

Wednesday 3	v	LEICESTER CITY	H
Sunday 7	v	SOUTHAMPTON	H
Sunday 14	v	BRADFORD CITY	A

Liverpool 0

VENUE: Anfield, 7.45pm

ATTENDANCE: 43,456

REFEREE: Graham Poll (Tring)

1 **WESTERVELD**

12 **HYYPIA**

2 **HENCHOZ**

21 **MATTEO**

23 **CARRAGHER**

11 **REDKNAPP**

25 **THOMPSON**

15 **BERGER**

16 **HAMANN**

8 **HESKEY**

10 **OWEN**

substitutes

4 **SONG**

19 **FRIEDEL**

24 **MURPHY**
(for 25) 74 mins

9 **FOWLER**
(for 16) 52 mins

22 **CAMARA**
(for 10) 66 mins

Leicester stunned the Kop by becoming the first visiting club for a quarter of a century to complete three successive Anfield wins and in the process dealt a massive blow to Liverpool's ambitions of qualifying for the Champions' League. Leeds, who beat Watford the same evening, leapfrogged Liverpool who had dropped from second to fourth in five days and had taken only one point from the last nine.

Jamie Redknapp and Robbie Savage show true commitment in their midfield battle.

Arsenal, back in 1975, had been the last team to topple Liverpool on three consecutive League visits to Anfield and Leicester took just one minute 58 seconds to signal their intention of emulating the Londoners. Neil Lennon pounced on a loose ball to provide Tony Cottee with a chance he took in clinical style, racing on to draw Sander Westerveld and fire past the Dutch goalkeeper before Stephane Henchoz or Jamie Carragher could rescue the situation.

The 34-year-old former Everton striker could not hide his delight. For Liverpool, however, it was the second game in succession they had been caught cold by an early goal.

They did respond swiftly. But club captain Jamie Redknapp, restored to the side in place of groin casualty Steven Gerrard for his first start since November, saw his free kick for Phil Gilchrist's

2 Leicester City

SCORERS: Cottee 2
Gilchrist 48

foul on Michael Owen seem destined for the top corner of the net until Pegguy Arphexad acrobatically diverted it for a corner.

Liverpool manager Gérard Houllier, who recalled David Thompson to the right of midfield in place of Danny Murphy, saw his team struggle to create openings as they were hustled and harried by a committed Leicester side who, as Worthington Cup winners, had already secured their European ticket in the UEFA Cup.

Robbie Savage played a major part in Leicester's victory. He epitomised the spirit of Martin O'Neill's team who deserved to win their third League match in succession at Anfield.

But they allowed Liverpool – including their £11 million 'old boy' Emile Heskey – little scope and early in the second half of a combative contest that at times threatened to boil over Liverpool were rocked when Leicester doubled their lead. Muzzy Izzet's corner glanced off Dominic Matteo's head for Gilchrist to apply the final touch for his first Leicester goal. A minute later Patrik Berger unleashed a 30-yard shot that beat Arphexad but crashed off the bar. But the former Lens keeper proceeded to make two fine saves from substitute Robbie Fowler – who replaced Dietmar Hamann – and also deny Berger and Redknapp.

Titi Camara and Murphy replaced Owen and Thompson but they could not prevent Liverpool's third consecutive outing without scoring. It was Liverpool's first home League defeat since Everton's win in September, leaving Houllier reflecting: 'Perhaps this game shows we are not ready for the Champions' League. We are going through a bad phase.'

ARPHEXAD 22
SINCLAIR 3
IMPEY 24
SAVAGE 14
ELLIOTT 18
GILCHRIST 15
GUPPY 11
LENNON 7
IZZET 6
COTTEE 27
EADIE 10

substitutes
FLOWERS 1
WALSH 5
20 **MARSHALL**
(for 27) 86 mins
29 **OAKES**
(for 10) 90 mins
ZAGORAKIS 37

> *'Liverpool's prospects of returning to the European arena where they were once classed as kings suffered a potentially fatal blow from serfs who make a habit of rising above their status.'*
> – *Derick Allsop, The* Independent

Liverpool | 0

VENUE: Anfield, 4.00pm

ATTENDANCE: 44,015

REFEREE: Paul Alcock (Redhill)

1 **WESTERVELD**

4 **SONG**

12 **HYYPIA**

2 **HENCHOZ**

21 **MATTEO**

23 **CARRAGHER**

11 **REDKNAPP**

15 **BERGER**

8 **HESKEY**

9 **FOWLER**

22 **CAMARA**

substitutes

18 **MEIJER**
(for 22) 80 mins

19 **FRIEDEL**

24 **MURPHY**

16 **HAMANN**
(for 4) 78 mins

25 **THOMPSON**
(for 9) 60 mins

Liverpool went into their final home League game of the season knowing that they were assured of a return to Europe. Chelsea's defeat by Arsenal the previous day meant that Anfield would at least host UEFA Cup football the following season.

'Last season we finished with nothing so what we have already achieved shows how much we have improved on that,' said manager Gérard Houllier.

But Liverpool faced Southampton still pursuing a Champions' League place and Houllier re-shaped his side in a bid to end the goal drought that had spanned three games .

He rested Michael Owen - omitting him from the 16 — and switched Dietmar Hamann and David Thompson to the bench. In came Robbie Fowler, for his first start since September, and Titi Camara who joined Emile Heskey in a three-pronged assault force. Jamie Carragher's switch to midfield meant a recall at right back for Rigobert Song.

Once again, however, Liverpool could not find the scoring formula. Indeed, in the first half they

Heskey needed all his speed and strength in this tough, penultimate game.

0 Southampton

Titi Camara worked hard to break the deadlock but, along with his colleagues, was unable to find a way through the Saints defence.

MOSS 13
DODD 2
EL KHALEJ 27
RICHARDS 6
BRIDGE 18
OAKLEY 8
DAVIES 10
TESSEM 21
SOLTVEDT 32
KACHLOUL 30
PAHARS 17

substitutes
MARSDEN 4
LUNDEKVAM 5
BENALI 15
RODRIGUES 19
BEVAN 20

had to thank Sander Westerveld for twice denying Southampton the lead.

The Dutch goalkeeper leaped magnificently to turn over a powerful Jo Tessem header from Hassan Kachloul's cross and then did likewise to keep out Kachloul's right-foot volley.

> *'We wanted to put more pressure on Leeds by winning today. But it wasn't to be. It's disappointing but, looking at the season as a whole, it's been a successful one for us.'* – Jamie Redknapp

Westerveld's anticipation and alterness again rescued Liverpool early in the second period when he raced out to block from Tessem in a one-on-one with the Norwegian.

Liverpool presented more of a threat after the interval with visiting keeper Neil Moss saving well from Fowler's shot on the turn and from Carragher's low, long range attempt .

Fowler was withdrawn after an hour of his major comeback with Thompson sent on and Heskey moving in from the flank to take a more central role. Camara had a shot saved and saw another fly wide before he was replaced by Erik Meijer, shortly after Hamann went on for Song.

Liverpool's best effort came three minutes from the end when centre back Stephane Henchoz made an attacking sortie to plant a header that grazed Moss's bar.

But referee Paul Alcock's final whistle meant that Liverpool had gone four games without a goal and taken only two points from 12. Yet the draw took them above Leeds into third place on goal difference and the Kop showed their feelings by chanting 'We Love You Liverpool' as the players did a farewell lap of the pitch.

Bradford City | 1

VENUE: Valley Parade, 4.00pm

ATTENDANCE: 18,276

REFEREE: Dermot Gallagher (Banbury)

SCORER: Wetherall 13

13 **CLARKE**
18 **HALLE**
14 **O'BRIEN**
5 **WETHERALL**
16 **SHARPE**
7 **LAWRENCE**
4 **MCCALL**
20 **DREYER**
11 **BEAGRIE**
15 **WINDASS**
28 **SAUNDERS**

substitutes

22 **JACOBS**
(for 11) 80 mins

19 **RANKIN**
(for 28) 78 mins

6 **WESTWOOD**

8 **BLAKE**

31 **DAVISON**

Bradford's desperate battle for survival in English football's top flight triumphed over Liverpool's bid for a Champions' League qualifying place on a warm, tense afternoon at Valley Parade.

The goal that decided the issue came – with fitting misfortune for Liverpool – in the 13th minute. David Wetherall was allowed to rise unchallenged to meet Gunnar Halle's free kick, conceded by Dietmar Hamman's foul on the Norwegian full back, and head powerfully past Sander Westerveld.

For Wetherall, it was a massive old pals' act for his former club Leeds, whose goalless draw at West Ham the same day meant that Liverpool had to beat Bradford to leapfrog the Elland Road club into third place. In the event, David O'Leary's side finished two points ahead of Gérard Houllier's team who had already qualified for the UEFA Cup.

Houllier recalled Steven Gerrard to central midfield with captain Jamie Redknapp switching to a right flank role while up front the manager paraded Michael Owen and Emile Heskey and omitted Robbie Fowler from the 16 for fitness reasons. But, overall, it was a disappointing, lacklustre

> *'It is unfair to pigeon-hole the way Liverpool have ended the campaign with all those others in the none-too-distant past when much was promised and the minimum eventually gained. A new team with new players has brought a new attitude and renewed hope for the future. The campaign, however, still leaves much for the manager to muse upon.'* – Paul Joyce, Liverpool Daily Post

Liverpool display and their failure to beat Matt Clarke in the home goal meant that they ended the campaign without scoring in five consecutive League games, the club's worst barren sequence since 1993.

Ten minutes before the interval Clarke crucially reached a Heskey delivery just before Owen. The Liverpool pair combined again to go even closer to equalising. Heskey flicked on a long ball from Gerrard into the path of Owen who raced past Clarke and Wetherall. But Owen's shot was cleared off the line by Halle.

In the second half, when Titi Camata, Vladimir Smicer and Erik Meijer replaced Gerrard, Patrik Berger and Dominic Matteo, Owen had a header turned over by Clarke and sent a shot narrowly off target. But at the other end home substitute Isaiah Rankin fired wide when clean through and then a long-distance chip from Dean Windass had Westerveld scrambling back to divert the ball away from the top corner of his net.

Referee Dermott Gallagher's final whistle sounded a note of deep frustration for Liverpool but signalled an explosion of ecstatic relief for Bradford, not least for their Liverpool-born manager

0 **Liverpool**

Paul Jewell, an Anfield reserve in the glory days of Bob Paisley. 'Only twice in my life have I wanted Liverpool to lose,' said Jewell. 'One was when we played at Anfield this season and they beat us. The second time was today. I'm proud of my players.'

Recalled Steven Gerrard's determination to win the ball is perfectly captured… but it was a disappointing last match of the season for the youngster and the rest of the Liverpool team.

WESTERVELD 1
CARRAGHER 23
HENCHOZ 2
HYYPIA 12
MATTEO 21
REDKNAPP 11
GERRARD 28
HAMANN 16
BERGER 15
HESKEY 8
OWEN 10

substitutes
MEIJER 18
(for 21) 81 mins
SMICER 7
(for 28) 60 mins
CAMARA 22
(for 15) 60 mins
SONG 4
NIELSEN 26

Despite his disappointment, Gérard Houllier expressed similar sentiments about his squad. 'It was a very sad way for us to end the season and we have paid for a difficult start and a weak finish. But it should not cloud the achievement of the lads. I'm very pleased with what they've done overall.'

Wednesday 3	v	LEICESTER CITY	H	0-2
Sunday 7	v	SOUTHAMPTON	H	0-0
Sunday 14	v	BRADFORD CITY	A	0-1

1

SANDER WESTERVELD

PLAYER OF THE MONTH

Sander Westerveld ended his first season in English football with a series of impressive saves in the final matches, including three memorable stops in the home duel with Southampton. The Dutch goalkeeper played in all but two of Liverpool's 38 Premiership games and played a key role in the club having the best defensive record in the division of just 30 goals conceded.

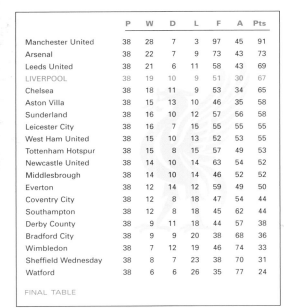

	P	W	D	L	F	A	Pts
Manchester United	38	28	7	3	97	45	91
Arsenal	38	22	7	9	73	43	73
Leeds United	38	21	6	11	58	43	69
LIVERPOOL	38	19	10	9	51	30	67
Chelsea	38	18	11	9	53	34	65
Aston Villa	38	15	13	10	46	35	58
Sunderland	38	16	10	12	57	56	58
Leicester City	38	16	7	15	55	55	55
West Ham United	38	15	10	13	52	53	55
Tottenham Hotspur	38	15	8	15	57	49	53
Newcastle United	38	14	10	14	63	54	52
Middlesbrough	38	14	10	14	46	52	52
Everton	38	12	14	12	59	49	50
Coventry City	38	12	8	18	47	54	44
Southampton	38	12	8	18	45	62	44
Derby County	38	9	11	18	44	57	38
Bradford City	38	9	9	20	38	68	36
Wimbledon	38	7	12	19	46	74	33
Sheffield Wednesday	38	8	7	23	38	70	31
Watford	38	6	6	26	35	77	24

FINAL TABLE

'Talking Points'

- 7/5/00 This was **only the second goalless draw** in all the League games between Liverpool and Southampton. **Robbie Fowler started his first game since the Merseyside derby back in September.**

- 7/5/00 **Liverpool fail to defeat Southampton for the third time** this season. **Both league games were drawn** and the Saints won the Worthington Cup encounter 2-1.

- 14/5/00 Bradford retained their Premiership status, while **Liverpool** had already **qualified for a UEFA Cup place.** Liverpool failed to score for the fifth successive game for the first time in the League since October 1993.

'Talking Points'

for more info visit www.liverpoolfc.net

season review

season review
first team

It was a backhanded compliment to Gérard Houllier and his players that their form over much of the season, which saw them climb to second place in the Premiership, sparked such high expectations that Liverpool's last-day failure to grasp a Champions' League qualifying place was draped in disappointment.

Yet fourth place – three positions higher than the previous season – a ticket into the UEFA Cup and the best defensive record in the top flight represent a solid advance even if the gloss was reduced by a goal drought over the final five games that was as inexplicable as it was surprising.

Strangely, Liverpool's fortunes during the season were polarised around the two Mersey derby games against Everton. The Anfield defeat by their neighbours in September meant that Liverpool, languishing in 12th place, had lost three of their first four home Premiership games.

As Houllier observed: 'Nobody at that stage would have expected us to be in a position at the end of the season where we were regretting not getting third place.'

But that is exactly what happened, with a march that matched that of runaway champions Manchester United. Liverpool responded to the Everton defeat by stringing together a League sequence of only two defeats in 25 games.

It brought them a harvest of 55 points up to their victory at Wimbledon in April and took them into second place for the first time in 19 months. Suddenly, though, the goals dried up with the first of five consecutive barren outings coming in the Goodison Park return with Everton on Good Friday.

That was followed by a couple of 2-0 defeats – at Chelsea and at home to Leicester – before a goalless home duel with Southampton and a 1-0 reverse at Bradford completed Liverpool's longest run without a goal since October 1993, during Graeme Souness's period as manager.

They closed with only two points from the final 15 but that anti-climax to the campaign, however, should not obscure Liverpool's progress on the field with a batch of newly-signed foreigners and prolonged injury absences by Robbie Fowler, Michael Owen, club captain Jame Redknapp and Czech Republic star Vladimir Smicer, one of Houllier's overseas captures.

The defence, for so long in the 1990's the weakness of Liverpool teams, at last looked a secure unit with Finnish giant Sami Hyypia and Swiss defender Stephane Henchoz forging an impressive centre back link in front of another new capture Sander Westerveld, the £4 million Dutch goalkeeper.

Liverpool conceded only 30 goals in their 38 Premiership games – 15 fewer than Manchester United – only for their tally at the other end to cost them dear. They could muster only 51 goals in the League. But if fate is kind to Fowler and Owen their potential link with £11 million record buy Emile Heskey could be goal-laden.

Gérard Houllier's determination to face the challenges looming in the 2000-2001 season was reflected in his summer transfer activity. The Liverpool manager signed his compatriot Bernard Diomede from Auxerre in a £3 million deal. The 26-year-old left flank raider, a member of France's triumphant 1998 World Cup squad, said: 'I am very happy to be joining a club with a French coach who I respect and know well.'

Houllier's squad was also set to be supplemented by the arrival of two more foreigners in German defender Markus Babbel from Bayern Munich and Guadeloupe-born French goalkeeper Pegguy Arphexad from Leicester as well as former Scotland captain Gary McAllister from Coventry, all three due to sign on free transfers under the Bosman ruling.

BACK ROW: Graham Carter (kit manager), Stephane Henchoz, Dietmar Hamann, Titi Camara, Karlheinz Riedle (now Fulham), Sander Westerveld, Jorgen Nielsen, Stephen Wright, Phil Babb, Vegard Heggem, Stig Inge Bjornebye, Gary Armer (masseur)

MIDDLE ROW: Joe Corrigan (goalkeeping coach), Patrice Bergues (coach), Steve Staunton, Frode Kippe, Vladimir Smicer, Patrik Berger, Rigobert Song, Bjorn Tore Kvarme (now St Etienne), Jon Newby, Erik Meijer, Sami Hyypia, Djimi Traore, Haukur Ingi Gudnason, Phil Thompson (assistant manager), Sammy Lee (coach)

FRONT ROW: David Thompson, Danny Murphy, Steven Gerrard, Jamie Redknapp (captain), Gérard Houllier (team manager), Robbie Fowler (vice-captain), Dominic Matteo, Jamie Carragher, Michael Owen

SAMI HYYPIA

12

MICHAEL OWEN

10

Appearances and Goalscorers 1999-2000

NAME	PREMIER LEAGUE		FA CUP		LEAGUE CUP		TOTAL	
	APPS	GOALS	APPS	GOALS	APPS	GOALS	APPS	GOALS
BERGER, Patrik	34	9	1	0	2	0	37	9
CAMARA, Titi	33	9	2	1	2	0	37	10
CARRAGHER, Jamie	36	0	2	0	2	0	40	0
FOWLER, Robbie	14	3	0	0	0	0	14	3
FRIEDEL, Brad	2	0	0	0	2	0	4	0
GERRARD, Steven	29	1	2	0	0	0	31	1
HAMANN, Dietmar	28	1	2	0	0	0	30	1
HEGGEM, Vegard	22	1	0	0	3	0	25	1
HENCHOZ, Stephane	29	0	2	0	2	0	33	0
HESKEY, Emile	12	3	0	0	0	0	12	3
HYYPIA, Sami	38	2	2	0	2	0	42	2
KIPPE, Frode	0	0	0	0	1	0	1	0
MATTEO, Dominic	32	0	2	1	0	0	34	1
MAXWELL, Layton	0	0	0	0	1	1	1	1
MEIJER, Erik	21	0	0	0	3	2	24	2
MURPHY, Danny	23	3	2	0	2	3	27	6
NEWBY, Jon	1	0	2	0	1	0	4	0
OWEN, Michael	27	11	1	0	2	1	30	12
REDKNAPP, Jamie	22	3	0	0	1	0	23	3
RIEDLE, Karlheinz	1	0	0	0	1	2	2	2
SMICER, Vladimir	21	1	2	0	2	0	25	1
SONG, Rigobert	18	0	1	0	2	0	21	0
STAUNTON, Steve	12	0	1	0	3	1	16	1
THOMPSON, David	27	3	1	0	3	0	31	3
TRAORE, Djimi	0	0	0	0	2	0	2	0
WESTERVELD, Sander	36	0	2	0	1	0	39	0

Attendances 1999-2000 (AWAY)

7/8/99	League	**Sheffield Wednesday**	34,853	26/12/99	League	**Newcastle Utd**	36,445
21/8/99	League	**Middlesbrough**	34,783	3/1/00	League	**Tottenham Hotspur**	36,044
23/8/99	League	**Leeds Utd**	39,703	15/1/00	League	**Watford**	21,367
14/9/99	L Cup R2 L1	**Hull City**	10,034	13/2/00	League	**Arsenal**	38,098
18/9/99	League	**Leicester City**	21,623	4/3/00	League	**Manchester Utd**	61,592
2/10/99	League	**Aston Villa**	39,217	18/3/00	League	**Derby County**	33,378
13/10/99	L Cup R3	**Southampton**	13,822	1/4/00	League	**Coventry City**	23,098
23/10/99	League	**Southampton**	15,241	16/4/00	League	**Wimbledon**	26,102
20/11/99	League	**Sunderland**	42,015	21/4/00	League	**Everton**	40,052
27/11/99	League	**West Ham Utd**	26,043	29/4/00	League	**Chelsea**	34,957
12/12/99	FA Cup R3	**Huddersfield Town**	23,678	14/5/00	League	**Bradford City**	18,276

Attendances 1999-2000 (HOME)

14/8/99	League	**Watford**	44,174	28/12/99	League	**Wimbledon**	44,107
28/8/99	League	**Arsenal**	44,886	10/1/00	FA Cup R4	**Blackburn Rovers**	32,839
11/9/99	League	**Manchester Utd**	44,929	22/1/00	League	**Middlesbrough**	44,324
21/9/99	L Cup R2 L2	**Hull City**	24,318	5/2/00	League	**Leeds Utd**	44,793
27/9/99	League	**Everton**	44,802	11/3/00	League	**Sunderland**	44,693
16/10/99	League	**Chelsea**	44,826	15/3/00	League	**Aston Villa**	43,615
27/10/99	League	**West Ham Utd**	44,012	25/3/00	League	**Newcastle Utd**	44,743
1/11/99	League	**Bradford City**	40,483	9/4/00	League	**Tottenham Hotspur**	44,536
6/11/99	League	**Derby County**	44,467	3/5/00	League	**Leicester City**	43,456
5/12/99	League	**Sheffield Wednesday**	42,517	7/5/00	League	**Southampton**	44,015
18/12/99	League	**Coventry City**	44,024				

A bumper crowd paid a fitting warm salute to Liverpool's marathon man Ronnie Moran at his testimonial against Celtic on an emotional Anfield evening in May. To mark the occasion Liverpool wore their exciting new strip for the first time after signing a record £21 million Premiership record sponsorship deal with Reebok, extending the club's agreement with the kit manufacturers for a further three seasons.

An attendance of 33,300 paid tribute to Ronnie, who served Liverpool for just under half a century as player, captain, coach of the junior, reserve and first teams and several stints as caretaker manager.

Some 12,000 Celtic fans joined the Kop in chanting Ronnie's name as the man himself, who worked alongside such greats as Bill Shankly, Bob Paisley, Joe Fagan and Kenny Dalglish, admitted: 'When I joined the club as a youngster in 1949 I could never have dreamed I'd spend so long at Anfield or experience a night like this. The memory of it will stay with me forever. It's just wonderful.'

Liverpool stars past and present were there to salute Ronnie, including Phil Neal, Alan Kennedy, Bruce Grobbelaar, David Johnson, Craig Johnston, Gary Gillespie, Ian Rush, Steve McMahon and Dave Hickson while the club's retiring executive vice chairman Peter Robinson was also applauded by the fans on his Anfield farewell.

A Liverpool team that included Robbie Fowler for the entire 90 minutes and Michael Owen as a second half substitute claimed an impressive 4-1 win through a brace of goals from Erik Meijer and others from David Thompson and Titi Camara.

Guest player Christian Dailly of Blackburn replied for the visitors before the evening was climaxed by Ronnie Moran walking out on the pitch with Anfield legend and Celtic director of operations Kenny Dalglish. 'This is a remarkable night in honour of a man who is different class,' said Kenny, to thunderous applause.

FRIDAY 16 JULY 1999

v GERMAN REGIONAL SELECT
(away, Oberstaufen) won: 8-0
Scorers: Fowler 3, Berger 2, Murphy, Camara, Heggem

TUESDAY 20 JULY 1999

v WOLVES
(away, Molineux) won: 2-0
Scorers: Fowler, Riedle

THURSDAY 22 JULY 1999

CARLSBERG CHALLENGE

v LINFIELD
(away, Windsor Park, Belfast) won: 4-0
Scorers: Murphy, Berger, Redknapp, Porter own goal

SATURDAY 24 JULY 1999

CARLSBERG CHALLENGE

v FEYENOORD
(away, Windsor Park, Belfast) won: 2-0
Scorers: Smicer, Camara **LIVERPOOL WON TOURNAMENT**

THURSDAY 29 JULY 1999

v VELERENGA
(away, Ullevaal Stadium, Oslo) won: 4-1
Scorers: Hamann, Meijer, Riedle, Haraldsen own goal

SATURDAY 31 JULY 1999

v BLACKBURN ROVERS
(away, Ewood Park) drawn: 2-2
Scorers: Fowler, Redknapp

TUESDAY 3 AUGUST 1999

v MANCHESTER CITY
(away, Maine Road) lost: 1-2
Scorers: Thompson

WEDNESDAY 18 OCTOBER 1999

DISASTER CHARITY MATCH

v OMAGH TOWN
(away, Omagh) won: 7-1
Scorers: Camara 2, Meijer 2, Smicer, Berger, Redknapp

WEDNESDAY 16 FEBRUARY 2000

CENTENARY GAME

v BOURNEMOUTH
(away, Dean Court) won: 4-0
Scorers: Partridge, Murphy, Berger, Camara

TUESDAY 16 MAY 2000

RONNIE MORAN TESTIMONIAL

v CELTIC
(home, Anfield) won: 4-1
Scorers: Thompson, Meijer 2, Camara

SUNDAY 21 MAY 2000

STEVE STAUNTON/ TONY CASCARINO JOINT TESTIMONIAL

v REPUBLIC OF IRELAND
(away, Lansdowne Road, Dublin) lost: 2-4
Scorers: Heskey, Owen

player profiles

Phil Babb

Position: Defender
Born: Lambeth, London
Birthdate: 30 November 1970
Date signed: 1 September 1994 from Coventry City – £3.6 million
Other clubs: Millwall, Bradford City, Coventry City, Tranmere Rovers (loan)
Senior Liverpool debut: 17 September 1994 at Old Trafford against Manchester United as substitute for Jan Molby – League
Debut in English Football: 4 September 1990 for Bradford City against Bury at Gigg Lane

6

		LEAGUE		FA CUP		LEAGUE CUP		EUROPE		OTHER		TOTAL	
1999-2000 SEASON	APPS GOALS	0	0	0	0	0	0	0	0	0	0	0	0
LIVERPOOL CAREER	APPS GOALS	128	1	12	0	16	0	14	0	0	0	170	1

Patrik Berger

Position: Midfield
Born: Prague, Czech Republic
Birthdate: 10 November 1973
Date signed: 1 August 1996 from Borussia Dortmund, Germany – £3.25 million
Other clubs: Slavia Prague, Borussia Dortmund
Senior Liverpool debut: 7 September 1996 at Anfield against Southampton as substitute for Stan Collymore – League
Debut in English Football: As above

15

		LEAGUE		FA CUP		LEAGUE CUP		EUROPE		OTHER		TOTAL	
1999-2000 SEASON	APPS GOALS	34	9	1	0	2	0	0	0	0	0	37	9
LIVERPOOL CAREER	APPS GOALS	111	25	6	0	9	2	14	4	0	0	140	31

Stig Inge Bjornebye

Position: Defender
Born: Elverum, Norway
Birthdate: 11 December 1969
Date signed: 15 December 1992 from Rosenborg, Norway – £600,000
Other clubs: Strammen, Kongsvinger, Rosenborg
Senior Liverpool debut: 19 December 1992 at Highfield Road against Coventry City – League
Debut in English Football: As above

20

		LEAGUE		FA CUP		LEAGUE CUP		EUROPE		OTHER		TOTAL	
1999-2000 SEASON	APPS GOALS	0	0	0	0	0	0	0	0	0	0	0	0
LIVERPOOL CAREER	APPS GOALS	139	2	13	0	16	0	16	2	0	0	184	4

Aboubacar 'Titi' Camara

Position: Forward
Born: Donka, Guinea
Birthdate: 17 November 1972
Date signed: 1 June 1999 from Marseilles, France – £2.8 million
Other clubs: St Etienne, Lens, Olympique Marseille
Senior Liverpool debut: 7 August 1999 at Hillsborough against Sheffield Wednesday – League
Debut in English Football: As above

22

		LEAGUE		FA CUP		LEAGUE CUP		EUROPE		OTHER		TOTAL	
1999-2000 SEASON	APPS GOALS	33	9	2	1	2	0	0	0	0	0	37	10
LIVERPOOL CAREER	APPS GOALS	33	9	2	1	2	0	0	0	0	0	37	10

23

Jamie Carragher

Position: Defender/Midfield
Born: Liverpool
Birthdate: 28 January 1978
Date signed: 9 October 1996 – from Trainee
Other clubs: None
Senior Liverpool debut: 8 January 1997 at The Riverside against Middlesbrough as substitute for Rob Jones – League Cup
Debut in English Football: As above

		LEAGUE		FA CUP		LEAGUE CUP		EUROPE		OTHER		TOTAL	
1999-2000 SEASON	APPS GOALS	36	0	2	0	2	0	0	0	0	0	40	0
LIVERPOOL CAREER	APPS GOALS	92	2	4	0	7	0	7	0	0	0	110	2

9

Robbie Fowler

Position: Forward
Born: Liverpool
Birthdate: 9 April 1975
Date signed: 23 April 1992 – from Trainee
Other clubs: None
Senior Liverpool debut: 22 September 1993 at Craven Cottage against Fulham – League Cup
Debut in English Football: As above

		LEAGUE		FA CUP		LEAGUE CUP		EUROPE		OTHER		TOTAL	
1999-2000 SEASON	APPS GOALS	14	3	0	0	0	0	0	0	0	0	14	3
LIVERPOOL CAREER	APPS GOALS	199	109	19	10	27	21	20	10	0	0	265	150

Brad Friedel

Position: Goalkeeper
Born: Lakewood, Ohio USA
Birthdate: 18 May 1971
Date signed: 23 December 1997 from Colombus Crew, USA – £1 million
Other clubs: Galatasaray, Brondby, Columbus Crew
Senior Liverpool debut: 28 February 1998 at Villa Park against Aston Villa – League
Debut in English Football: As above

19

		LEAGUE		FA CUP		LEAGUE CUP		EUROPE		OTHER		TOTAL	
1999-2000 SEASON	APPS GOALS	2	0	0	0	2	0	0	0	0	0	4	0
LIVERPOOL CAREER	APPS GOALS	25	0	0	0	4	0	2	0	0	0	31	0

Steven Gerrard

Position: Midfield/Defender
Born: Whiston
Birthdate: 30 May 1980
Date signed: 26 February 1998 – from Trainee
Other clubs: None
Senior Liverpool debut: 29 November 1998 at Anfield against Blackburn Rovers as substitute for Vegard Heggem – League
Debut in English Football: As above

28

		LEAGUE		FA CUP		LEAGUE CUP		EUROPE		OTHER		TOTAL	
1999-2000 SEASON	APPS GOALS	29	1	2	0	0	0	0	0	0	0	31	1
LIVERPOOL CAREER	APPS GOALS	41	1	2	0	0	0	1	0	0	0	44	1

Dietmar Hamann

Position: Midfield
Born: Waldsasson, Germany
Birthdate: 27 August 1973
Date signed: 22 July 1999 from Newcastle United – £8 million
Other clubs: FC Wacker Munchen, Bayern Munich, Newcastle United
Senior Liverpool debut: 7 August 1999 at Hillsborough against Sheffield Wednesday – League
Debut in English Football: 15 August 1998 at St James' Park for Newcastle United against Charlton Athletic

16

		LEAGUE		FA CUP		LEAGUE CUP		EUROPE		OTHER		TOTAL	
1999-2000 SEASON	APPS GOALS	28	1	2	0	0	0	0	0	0	0	30	1
LIVERPOOL CAREER	APPS GOALS	28	1	2	0	0	0	0	0	0	0	30	1

Vegard Heggem

Position: Defender
Born: Trondheim, Norway
Birthdate: 13 July 1975
Date signed: 21 July 1998 from Rosenborg, Norway – £3.5 million
Other clubs: Rennebu Orkdal, Rosenborg
Senior Liverpool debut: 16 August 1998 at The Dell against Southampton – League
Debut in English Football: As above

14

		LEAGUE		FA CUP		LEAGUE CUP		EUROPE		OTHER		TOTAL	
1999-2000 SEASON	APPS GOALS	22	1	0	0	3	0	0	0	0	0	25	1
LIVERPOOL CAREER	APPS GOALS	51	3	1	0	4	0	5	0	0	0	61	3

Stephane Henchoz

Position: Defender
Born: Billens, Switzerland
Birthdate: 7 September 1974
Date signed: 2 July 1999 from Blackburn Rovers – £3.5m
Other clubs: Stade Payerne Bulle, Neuchatel Xamax, Hamburg, Blackburn Rovers
Senior Liverpool debut: 21 September 1999 at Boothferry Park against Hull City – League Cup
Debut in English football: 9 August 1997 at Ewood Park for Blackburn Rovers against Derby County

2

		LEAGUE		FA CUP		LEAGUE CUP		EUROPE		OTHER		TOTAL	
1999-2000 SEASON	APPS GOALS	29	0	2	0	2	0	0	0	0	0	33	0
LIVERPOOL CAREER	APPS GOALS	29	0	2	0	2	0	0	0	0	0	33	0

Emile Heskey

Position: Forward
Born: Leicester
Birthdate: 11 January 1978
Date signed: 10 March 2000 from Leicester City – £11m
Other clubs: Leicester City
Senior Liverpool debut: 11 March 2000 at Anfield against Sunderland – League
Debut in English football: 8 March 1995 at Loftus Road for Leicester City against Queens Park Rangers

8

		LEAGUE		FA CUP		LEAGUE CUP		EUROPE		OTHER		TOTAL	
1999-2000 SEASON	APPS GOALS	12	3	0	0	0	0	0	0	0	0	12	3
LIVERPOOL CAREER	APPS GOALS	12	3	0	0	0	0	0	0	0	0	12	3

Sami Hyypia

Position: Defender
Born: Porvoo, Finland
Birthdate: 7 October 1973
Date signed: 1 July 1999 from Willem II Tilburg, Holland – £2.6m
Other clubs: Pallo-Pelkot, Ku Mu, My Pa Anjalankoski, Willem II
Senior Liverpool debut: 7 August 1999 at Hillsborough against Sheffield Wednesday – League
Debut in English football: As above

12

		LEAGUE		FA CUP		LEAGUE CUP		EUROPE		OTHER		TOTAL	
1999-2000 SEASON	**APPS GOALS**	38	2	2	0	2	0	0	0	0	0	42	2
LIVERPOOL CAREER	**APPS GOALS**	38	2	2	0	2	0	0	0	0	0	42	2

Frode Kippe

Position: Defender/Midfield
Born: Oslo, Norway
Birthdate: 17 January 1978
Date signed: 6 January 1999 from Lillestrom, Norway – £700,000
Other clubs: Lillestrom, Stoke City (loan)
Senior Liverpool debut: 21 September 1999 at Anfield against Hull City as substitute for Vladimir Smicer – League Cup
Debut in English football: As above

31

		LEAGUE		FA CUP		LEAGUE CUP		EUROPE		OTHER		TOTAL	
1999-2000 SEASON	**APPS GOALS**	0	0	0	0	1	0	0	0	0	0	1	0
LIVERPOOL CAREER	**APPS GOALS**	0	0	0	0	1	0	0	0	0	0	1	0

21

Dominic Matteo

Position: Defender
Born: Dumfries, Scotland
Birthdate: 24 April 1974
Date signed: 27 May, 1992 – from Trainee
Other clubs: Sunderland (loan)
Senior Liverpool debut: 23 October 1993 at Maine Road against Manchester City – League
Debut in English football: As above

		LEAGUE		FA CUP		LEAGUE CUP		EUROPE		OTHER		TOTAL	
1999-2000 SEASON	APPS GOALS	32	0	2	1	0	0	0	0	0	0	34	1
LIVERPOOL CAREER	APPS GOALS	127	1	8	1	9	0	11	0	0	0	155	2

33

Layton Maxwell

Position: Midfield
Born: St Asaph, Wales
Birthdate: 3 October 1979
Date signed: 8 July 1996
Other clubs: None
Senior Liverpool debut: 21 September 1999 at Anfield against Hull City – League Cup
Debut in English football: As above

		LEAGUE		FA CUP		LEAGUE CUP		EUROPE		OTHER		TOTAL	
1999-2000 SEASON	APPS GOALS	0	0	0	0	1	1	0	0	0	0	1	1
LIVERPOOL CAREER	APPS GOALS	0	0	0	0	1	1	0	0	0	0	1	1

Erik Meijer

Position: Forward
Born: Meersen, Holland
Birthdate: 2 August 1969
Date signed: 1 July 1999 from Bayer Leverkusen, Germany – Bosman Ruling
Other clubs: Fortuna Sittard MVV, PSV Eindhoven, KFC Verdingen, Bayer Leverkusen
Senior Liverpool debut: 7 August 1999 at Hillsborough against Sheffield Wednesday as substitute for Titi Camara – League
Debut in English football: As above

18

		LEAGUE		FA CUP		LEAGUE CUP		EUROPE		OTHER		TOTAL	
1999-2000 SEASON	APPS GOALS	21	0	0	0	3	2	0	0	0	0	24	2
LIVERPOOL CAREER	APPS GOALS	21	0	0	0	3	2	0	0	0	0	24	2

Danny Murphy

Position: Midfield
Born: Chester
Birthdate: 18 March 1977
Date signed: 15 July 1997 from Crewe Alexandra – £1.5m
Other clubs: Crewe Alexandra
Senior Liverpool debut: 9 August 1997 at Selhurst Park against Wimbledon as substitute for Stig Inge Bjornebye – League
Debut in English football: 11 December 1993 at Layer Road for Crewe Alexandra against Colchester United

24

		LEAGUE		FA CUP		LEAGUE CUP		EUROPE		OTHER		TOTAL	
1999-2000 SEASON	APPS GOALS	23	3	2	0	2	3	0	0	0	0	27	6
LIVERPOOL CAREER	APPS GOALS	40	3	3	0	4	3	1	0	0	0	48	6

32

Jon Newby

Position: Midfield
Born: Warrington
Birthdate: 28 November 1978
Date signed: 28 May 1997 from – from Trainee
Other clubs: Crewe Alexandra (loan)
Senior Liverpool debut: 21 September 1999 at Anfield against Hull City as substitute for
Stephane Henchoz – League Cup
Debut in English football: As above

		LEAGUE		FA CUP		LEAGUE CUP		EUROPE		OTHER		TOTAL	
1999-2000 SEASON	**APPS** GOALS	1	0	2	0	1	0	0	0	0	0	4	0
LIVERPOOL CAREER	**APPS** GOALS	1	0	2	0	1	0	0	0	0	0	4	0

26

Jorgen Nielsen

Position: Goalkeeper
Born: Nykabing, Denmark
Birthdate: 6 May 1971
Date signed: 26 March 1997 from Hvidovre, Denmark – £400,000
Other clubs: Lillestrom, Hvidovre
Senior Liverpool debut: N/A
Debut in English football: N/A

		LEAGUE		FA CUP		LEAGUE CUP		EUROPE		OTHER		TOTAL	
1999-2000 SEASON	**APPS** GOALS	0	0	0	0	0	0	0	0	0	0	0	0
LIVERPOOL CAREER	**APPS** GOALS	0	0	0	0	0	0	0	0	0	0	0	0

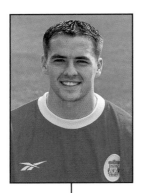

Michael Owen

Position: Forward
Born: Chester
Birthdate: 14 December 1979
Date signed: 18 December 1996 – from Trainee
Other clubs: None
Senior Liverpool debut: 6 May 1997 at Selhurst Park against Wimbledon as substitute for
Patrick Berger – League
Debut in English football: As above

10

		LEAGUE		FA CUP		LEAGUE CUP		EUROPE		OTHER		TOTAL	
		APPS	GOALS	APPS	GOALS	APPS	GOALS	APPS	GOALS	APPS	GOALS	APPS	GOALS
1999-2000 SEASON	APPS GOALS	27	11	1	0	2	1	0	0	0	0	30	12
LIVERPOOL CAREER	APPS GOALS	95	48	3	2	8	6	10	3	0	0	116	59

Jamie Redknapp

Position: Midfield
Born: Barton-on-Sea
Birthdate: 25 June 1973
Date signed: 14 January 1991 from Bournemouth – £350,000
Other clubs: Bournemouth
Senior Liverpool debut: 23 October 1991 at Auxerre, France against Auxerre – UEFA Cup
Debut in English football: 13 January 1990 at Boothferry Park for Bournemouth against Hull City

11

		LEAGUE		FA CUP		LEAGUE CUP		EUROPE		OTHER		TOTAL	
		APPS	GOALS	APPS	GOALS	APPS	GOALS	APPS	GOALS	APPS	GOALS	APPS	GOALS
1999-2000 SEASON	APPS GOALS	22	3	0	0	1	0	0	0	0	0	23	3
LIVERPOOL CAREER	APPS GOALS	233	29	18	2	26	5	23	3	0	0	300	39

Vladimir Smicer

Position: Midfield/Forward
Born: Degin, Czech Republic
Birthdate: 24 May 1973
Date signed: 1 July 1999 from Lens, France – £3.75m
Other clubs: Slavia Prague, Lens
Senior Liverpool debut: 7 August at Hillsborough against Sheffield Wednesday – League
Debut in English football: As above

7

		LEAGUE		FA CUP		LEAGUE CUP		EUROPE		OTHER		TOTAL	
1999-2000 SEASON	APPS GOALS	21	1	2	0	2	0	0	0	0	0	25	1
LIVERPOOL CAREER	APPS GOALS	21	1	2	0	2	0	0	0	0	0	25	1

Rigobert Song

Position: Defender
Born: Nkenlicock, Cameroon
Birthdate: 1 July 1976
Date signed: 22 January 1999 from Salernitana, Italy – £2.6m
Other clubs: Tonnerre Yaounde, Metz, Salernitana
Senior Liverpool debut: 30 January 1999 at Highfield Road against Coventry City – League
Debut in English football: As above

4

		LEAGUE		FA CUP		LEAGUE CUP		EUROPE		OTHER		TOTAL	
1999-2000 SEASON	APPS GOALS	18	0	1	0	2	0	0	0	0	0	21	0
LIVERPOOL CAREER	APPS GOALS	31	0	1	0	2	0	0	0	0	0	34	0

5

Steve Staunton

Position: Defender
Born: Drogheda, Republic of Ireland
Birthdate: 19 January 1969
Date signed: (Spell one) 2 September 1986 from Dundalk, Republic of Ireland – £20,000
(Spell two) 2 July 1998 from Aston Villa – Bosman Ruling
Other clubs: Dundalk, Bradford City (loan), Aston Villa
Senior Liverpool debut: 17 September 1988 at Anfield against Tottenham Hotspur as a
substitute for Jan Molby – League
Debut in English football: 14 November 1987 at Valley Parade for Bradford City against
Sheffield United

		LEAGUE		FA CUP		LEAGUE CUP		EUROPE		OTHER		TOTAL	
1999-2000 SEASON	APPS GOALS	12	0	1	0	3	1	0	0	0	0	16	1
LIVERPOOL CAREER	APPS GOALS	108	0	18	1	13	5	6	0	1	1	146	7

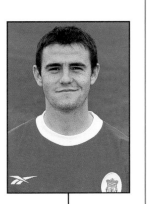

25

David Thompson

Position: Midfield
Born: Birkenhead
Birthdate: 12 September 1977
Date signed: 8 November 1994 – from Trainee
Other clubs: Swindon Town (loan)
Senior Liverpool debut: 19 August 1996 at Anfield against Arsenal as a substitute for
Robbie Fowler – League
Debut in English football: As above

		LEAGUE		FA CUP		LEAGUE CUP		EUROPE		OTHER		TOTAL	
1999-2000 SEASON	APPS GOALS	27	3	1	0	3	0	0	0	0	0	31	3
LIVERPOOL CAREER	APPS GOALS	48	5	1	0	5	0	2	0	0	0	56	5

30

Djimi Traore

Position: Defender
Born: Laval, France
Birthdate: 1 March 1980
Date signed: 18 February 1999 from Laval, France – £550,000
Other clubs: Laval
Senior Liverpool debut: 14 September 1999 at Boothferry Park against Hull City – League Cup
Debut in English football: As above

		LEAGUE		FA CUP		LEAGUE CUP		EUROPE		OTHER		TOTAL	
1999-2000 SEASON	APPS GOALS	0	0	0	0	2	0	0	0	0	0	2	0
LIVERPOOL CAREER	APPS GOALS	0	0	0	0	2	0	0	0	0	0	2	0

1

Sander Westerveld

Position: Goalkeeper
Born: Enschede, Holland
Birthdate: 23 October 1974
Date signed: 15 June 1999 from Vitesse Arnhem, Holland – £4 million
Other clubs: FC Twente, Vitesse Arnhem
Senior Liverpool debut: 7 August 1999 at Hillsborough against Sheffield Wednesday – League
Debut in English Football: As above

		LEAGUE		FA CUP		LEAGUE CUP		EUROPE		OTHER		TOTAL	
1999-2000 SEASON	APPS GOALS	36	0	2	0	1	0	0	0	0	0	39	0
LIVERPOOL CAREER	APPS GOALS	36	0	2	0	1	0	0	0	0	0	39	0

29

Stephen Wright

Position: Defender
Born: Liverpool
Birthdate: 8 February 1980
Date signed: 8 July 1996
Other clubs: Crewe Alexandra (loan)
Senior Liverpool debut: N/A
Debut in English football: N/A

		LEAGUE		FA CUP		LEAGUE CUP		EUROPE		OTHER		TOTAL	
1999-2000 SEASON	APPS GOALS	0	0	0	0	0	0	0	0	0	0	0	0
LIVERPOOL CAREER	APPS GOALS	0	0	0	0	0	0	0	0	0	0	0	0

reserves

JOE'S SPECIAL RESERVES RESTORE THE GLITTER

Liverpool reserves landed their first championship for a decade to signal what everyone at Anfield hopes is a positive omen for the senior side in their next Premiership campaign.

The club's second team, guided by former England and Manchester City goalkeeper Joe Corrigan, lifted a new trophy by storming to the title of the inaugural FA Premier Reserve League (North). It is the first time since 1990 that Liverpool reserves have won their championship. The last time was when they played in the Pontins Central League and were coached by Phil Thompson, now assistant to manager Gérard Houllier. That reserve title win coincided with Kenny Dalglish's side landing Liverpool's last League championship and coach Corrigan believes that the foundation is right for the club to challenge once more for the big prizes.

'I think the achievement of the reserve team is down to the boss's attitude, because he wants success at all levels of the club,' said Joe, who arrived at Liverpool as goalkeeping coach six years ago and has been coaching the reserves for two seasons.

He added: 'Sammy Lee was in charge of the reserves before me and the boss has made the job a bit easier for me. He has made it plain to everyone at the club that he wants them playing football. So if a player is not involved in the first team he has to play games at another level.

'Nobody is allowed to just kick their heels. Everybody has to play to prove their fitness and prove themselves good enough to appear for Liverpool Football Club and Gerard and Phil watch many of the reserve games to provide even greater motivation for players to perform well.

'I don't think it's any coincidence that the first team and the reserves both did well in the past season. The reserves were second in the Pontins League the season before last and won the championship of a stronger league last season. Likewise, the first team has also made progress.

'In fact, last season was a fantastic experience for the reserves because with the new league composed of clubs with Premiership status our lads, especially the youngsters, have had the benefit of playing against better quality players than previously.'

Liverpool, who staged seven of their home reserve games at Knowsley Road, St Helens, lost just once – a 3-0 February reverse at Sunderland – conceded only 16 goals and used 44 players en route to clinching the reserve championship with three games to spare.

Joe added: 'We had some great games but the one that sticks in my mind is our match at Newcastle in January when, apart from goalkeeper Jorgen Nielsen, our oldest player was 19.

'Newcastle played six or seven internationals yet we beat them 1-0. A week later we went up there for the away fixture and beat them again, this time 2-0.

'The thing that has pleased all the staff, the boss, Phil Thompson, Patrice Bergues, Sammy and me, has been the response of all the players. Those who have not been in the first team for

whatever reason have come into the reserves, buckled down and done a job. That's to the great credit of everybody.

'When we were getting close to winning the reserve league it wasn't just our regular players, like Jon Newby, Djimi Traore and Layton Maxwell, who were counting down and checking how many points we needed to be sure.

'Michael Owen, Sami Hyypia and other first teamers were also keen to know and that is a reflection of the attitude the boss has instilled. I remember a quote from the great Bill Shankly from the days when I first started playing football.

'He said: "The success of the first team is the happiness of the reserves." It's been proved with the Liverpool of old and Manchester United in recent years. Success does breed success and, hopefully, those days are coming back to Liverpool.

'We've also had kids coming from our Academy who have been working with Sammy and Patrice and stepping up into the reserves. That's good to see, too. John Miles and Ian Armstrong, for example, have been particularly impressive.

'Being responsible for the reserves has been a fantastic experience for me. It was an honour to be given the job and I'm delighted at how well the players have performed. I'm grateful for the wonderful assistance from the other members of staff and that includes physios Mark Browes and John Wright. It's a team effort all the way through.'

v MIDDLESBROUGH (home) drawn: 1-1

Friedel, Song, Kvarme, Traore, Staunton, Newby (N Murphy 83), Maxwell, D Murphy, Babb, Meijer (49), **Riedle**

Subs: Hogg, Foley, Navarro, Otsemobor, McIlroy, Gudnason

v LEEDS UNITED (away) won: 3-1

Friedel, N Murphy, Bjornebye, Jones, Maxwell (Navarro), Traore, Newby **(Armstrong), D Murphy,** Riedle **(Miles),** Meijer, **Partridge**

Subs: Nielsen, Boardman

v ASTON VILLA (away) drawn: 1-1

Nielsen, N Murphy, Bjornebye, Jones, Traore, Maxwell (Newby), Matteo (Navarro), D Murphy, Riedle (14), **Meijer, Camara, (Partridge)**

Subs:

v MANCHESTER UNITED (home) drawn: 0-0

Friedel, N Murphy (Boardman), Kippe, Henchoz, Bjornebye, Maxwell, Navarro, Partridge, Arnarsson (Olsen), Newby, Armstrong

Subs: Dunbavin, Gudnason, Jones

v SHEFFIELD WEDNESDAY (away) won: 2-1

Friedel, Song, Traore, Henchoz, (N Murphy), Kippe, Gerrard, Thompson, D Murphy, Meijer **(Newby),** Camara, **Maxwell, (Partridge)**

Subs: Dunbavin, O'Mara

v EVERTON (away) won: 2-0

Friedel, Navarro, Traore, Jones (N Murphy), Matteo, Thompson (Newby), D Murphy, **Bjornebye, Maxwell (Olsen), Camara,** Meijer

Subs: Dunbavin, Miles

v BOLTON WANDERERS (away) won: 4-0

Nielsen, N Murphy (Partridge), Traore, Wright, **Matteo, Bjornbye, Newby, Navarro,** Meijer 3, **Maxwell, Miles (Armstrong)**

Subs: Dunbavin, Jones

TUESDAY 16 NOVEMBER 1999

v SUNDERLAND (home, Knowsley Road) won: 4-0

Westerveld, Song, Matteo, Henchoz (Maxwell), Hyypia (Traore), Gerrard, Thompson, Carragher, Fowler (Meijer), Murphy, Berger

Subs: Nielsen, Bjornebye

MONDAY 22 NOVEMBER 1999

v BARNSLEY (away) won: 6-2

Nielsen, Heggem, Traore, Babb, Kippe, Bjornebye, Thompson (Navarro), Fowler 3, Carragher, Meijer (Newby 2), Maxwell

Subs: Dunbavin, N Murphy, Gudnason

WEDNESDAY 1 DECEMBER 1999

v BLACKBURN ROVERS (home, Knowsley Road) drawn: 3-3

Friedel, Navarro, Staunton (Partridge), Babb, Kippe, Maxwell, Newby 2, Carragher, Fowler (Gudnason), Camara (O'Mara), Bjornebye

Subs: Murphy, Nielsen

MONDAY 6 DECEMBER 1999

v ASTON VILLA (home, Knowsley Road) won: 3-1

Nielsen, Heggem, Staunton, Carragher (Traore), Kippe, Bjornebye (Partridge), Newby, Smicer (Murphy), Meijer, Navarro, Maxwell

Subs: Crookes, Olsen

TUESDAY 11 JANUARY 2000

v LEEDS UNITED (home, Knowsley Road) drawn: 1-1

Weber, Heggem (Murphy), Staunton, Jones, Traore, Navarro, Thompson, Maxwell, Newby, Miles (Armstrong) (C Thompson), Partridge

Subs: Dunbavin, O'Mara

MONDAY 17 JANUARY 2000

v NEWCASTLE UNITED (home) won: 1-0

Nielsen, N Murphy, O'Mara, Jones, Traore, Navarro, Partridge, Maxwell, Newby, Miles (Armstrong), Olsen (Thompson)

Subs: Gudnason, Crookes, Torpey

MONDAY 24 JANUARY 2000

v NEWCASTLE UNITED (away) won: 2-0

Friedel, N Murphy, Staunton, Jones, Traore, Navarro, Partridge, D Murphy, Newby, Maxwell, Camara 2 (Gudnason)

Subs: O'Mara, Parry, Boardman, Coupe, Beck, Morton

MONDAY 31 JANUARY 2000

v BOLTON WANDERERS (home, Knowsley Road) won: 5-1

Friedel, (Crookes), Heggem (N Murphy), Staunton, Jones, Traore, Navarro, Partridge,
D. Murphy 2, Meijer (Armstrong), Newby 2, Maxwell, Bolton own goal

Subs: Miles, Boardman, Thompson

TUESDAY 8 FEBRUARY 2000

v BRADFORD CITY (home, Knowsley Road) won: 4-0

Nielsen, Heggem, Staunton, Jones, Traore, Maxwell 2, Partridge, Murphy (Armstrong), Navarro,
Newby (Gudnason), Olsen (O'Mara)

Subs: Crookes, Thompson, Park

MONDAY 14 FEBRUARY 2000

v SUNDERLAND (away) lost: 0-3

Nielsen, Cavanagh, Bjornebye, Jones, Traore, Navarro, Partridge, Gudnason (Thompson), Miles,
Maxwell, O'Mara

Subs: Crookes, Culshaw, Beck, Park, Porter, Otsemobor

MONDAY 21 FEBRUARY 2000

v BARNSLEY (home, Knowsley Road) won: 3-0

Nielsen, Navarro, Matteo (Jones), Hyypia, Traore, Maxwell, Newby, Murphy,
Meijer (Armstrong), Camara (Miles), Bjornebye

Subs: Crookes, Boardman, Gudnason, Olsen

MONDAY 28 FEBRUARY 2000

v MIDDLESBROUGH (away) won: 2-0

Friedel, N Murphy, Bjornebye, Jones, Traore, Navarro, Partridge, Redknapp (pen) (Olsen),
Newby, Miles (Armstrong), Maxwell

Subs: Parry, Gudnason, Porter, Park

WEDNESDAY 8 MARCH 2000

v BLACKBURN ROVERS (away) drawn: 1-1

Nielsen, Navarro, Bjornebye, Traore, Staunton, Gerrard (N Murphy), Partridge, Redknapp,
D Murphy (Miles), Owen (pen), Maxwell (Armstrong)

Subs: Crookes, Gudnason, Jones, O'Mara

MONDAY 27 MARCH 2000

v SHEFFIELD WEDNESDAY (home) won: 1-0

Friedel, N Murphy, Traore, Song, Kippe, Navarro (Miles), Partridge (O'Mara), D Murphy, Meijer,
Maxwell, Redknapp (Thompson)

Subs: Crookes, O'Mara, Gudnason, Docherty

TUESDAY 11 APRIL 2000

v BRADFORD CITY (away) won: 2-0

Nielsen, Heggem, Traore, Song, Kippe, Navarro, Smicer (Miles), Camara, Fowler (Newby), Meijer, Redknapp (Maxwell)

Subs: Crookes, Partridge, Docherty, Olsen

MONDAY 17 APRIL 2000

v MANCHESTER UNITED (away) won: 2-0

Friedel, Heggem, Staunton (Navarro), Traore, Kippe, Murphy, Smicer (Newby), Redknapp, Fowler (Miles), Meijer, Camara

Subs: Maxwell, Partridge, Crookes

MONDAY 15 MAY 2000

LAYTON MAXWELL

33

JON NEWBY

32

v EVERTON (home) drawn: 2-2

Nielsen, Wright, Traore, Docherty (Murphy 46), Kippe (O'Mara 73), Navarro, Partridge (McIlroy 68), Maxwell, Newby, Miles, Olsen

Subs: Crooks, O'Brien

NAME	APPS	GOALS	NAME	APPS	GOALS
ARMSTRONG, Ian	8	0	McILROY, Brian	1	0
ARNARSSON, Viktor	1	0	MEIJER, Erik	14	7
BABB, Phil	3	0	MILES, John	11	1
BERGER, Patrik	1	0	MURPHY, Danny	12	5
BJORNEBYE, Stig	12	1	MURPHY, Neil	17	0
BOARDMAN, John	1	0	NAVARRO, Alan	21	1
CAMARA, Titi	8	5	NEWBY, Jon	19	12
CARRAGHER, Jamie	4	0	NIELSEN, Jorgen	11	0
CAVANAGH, Peter	1	0	OLSEN, James	6	1
CROOKES, Peter	1	0	O'MARA, Paul	6	0
DOCHERTY, Kevin	1	0	OWEN, Michael	1	1
FOWLER, Robbie	5	6	PARTRIDGE, Ritchie	17	1
FREIDEL, Brad	11	0	REDKNAPP, Jamie	5	2
GERRARD, Steven	3	1	RIEDLE, Karl Heinz	3	2
GUDNASON, Haukur	4	0	SMICER, Vladimir	3	1
HEGGEM, Vegard	7	1	SONG, Rigobert	5	0
HENCHOZ, Stepphane	3	0	STAUNTON, Steve	9	0
HYYPIA, Sami	2	0	THOMPSON, Dave	5	1
JONES, Eifion	10	0	THOMPSON, Chris	4	0
KIPPE, Frode	9	1	TIAORE, Djimi	22	0
KVARME, Bjorn	1	0	WEBER, Heinz	1	0
MATTEO, Dominic	5	0	WESTERVELD, Sander	1	0
MAXWELL, Layton	23	3	WRIGHT, Stephen	2	1

the academy

SPOTLIGHT ON THE JUNIORS

Liverpool's trail-blazing Academy, admired the world over for its facilities and opportunities for youngsters, has produced several players who have graduated to training with the seniors at Melwood. Under-19 coach Hughie McAuley has been enouraged by the past year's work at the £12 million Kirkby centre where Steve Heighway is director and Dave Shannon and Paul Lever guide the Under-17 and Under-14 teams. 'There is always room for improvement but the teams had a satisfactory season in their leagues and our main priority is to see players progressing here to the stage where they are ready to make the switch to Melwood,' said Hughie. 'In the past year we've had Alan Navarro and John Miles moving to Melwood and they follow Steven Gerrard, Stephen Wright, Jon Newby, Richie Partridge and Layton Maxwell. We hope that Ian Armstrong, Chris O'Brien and Stephen Warnock will make the switch next season when they will still be under 19.

'We have to consider if a boy is physically ready to handle the move to Melwood and train with senior players. But there's now a nice nucleus of players there who have come from the Academy over the past two years.'They're still developing and they've still got a lot to do but there's nobody better than the Melwood coaching staff to bring out the extra that lads require to get anywhere near our first team. Steven Gerrard, of course, has already made a big impact at first team level but we're looking to one or two others to start knocking on the door, too.

'We find that most of our Academy intake are local boys, although we do take one or two from outside. We are ready to welcome anybody from anywhere in the world and have already had some foreign lads here. Our scouts have their nets cast worldwide. We have to keep the doors open because we need the best players at the Academy.

'They start here at the age of seven in the community programme and can sign on at nine. We put a lot of work into bringing up those boys to the age of 16 when they become full time. Another positive factor about the Academy, which I think is often overlooked, is that even if players fall short of Liverpool's very high standards then there is a fair chance they can earn a living in football elsewhere. There are examples of such players dotted around the leagues.They have had the benefit of their time with us.'

Sports Minister Kate Hoey was one of many impressed visitors to the Academy. In January she unveiled sculptor Tom Murphy's specially commissioned work featuring three players in action, entitled 'Reach', which stands outside the 45-acre centre. Inside she officially opened the Ian Frodsham Indoor Soccer Arena, named after the club's former player who tragically lost a battle against cancer five years earlier at the age of 19.

the squad

back (l-r)

ALAN **NAVARRO**

STEPHEN **TORPEY**

STEPHEN **WARNOCK**

ALAN **COUPE**

MATTHEW **HOGG**

STEPHEN **GRACE**

PETER **CROOKES**

MATTY **PARRY**

CHRIS **THOMPSON**

JOHN **MILES**

IAN **ARMSTRONG**

PAUL **CULSHAW**

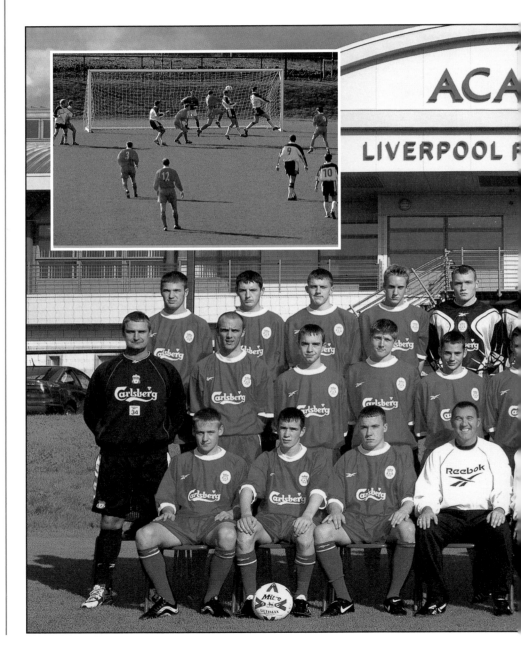

SIMON **FARNWORTH**
(PHYSIO)

EIFION **JONES**

ANTHONY **MORTON**

NEIL **MELLOR**

RICHIE **PARTRIDGE**

PAUL **O'MARA**

JOHN **BOARDMAN**

PETER **CAVANAGH**

BRIAN **MCILROY**

MICHAEL **FOLEY**

KEVIN **DOCHERTY**

BILLY **STEWART**

front (l-r)

STEPHEN **PORTER**

NEIL **PRINCE**

STEPHEN **PARK**

HUGHIE **MCAULEY**
(U-19 COACH)

STEVE **HEIGHWAY**
(ACADEMY DIRECTOR)

DAVE **SHANNON**
(U-17 COACH)

LEE **BECK**

JAMES **OLSEN**

CHRIS **O'BRIEN**

STEVE HEIGHWAY

HUGHIE McAULEY

DAVE SHANNON

STEVE HEIGHWAY – ACADEMY DIRECTOR

Liverpool's seventies star and Irish forward now oversees an operation which caters for 150 youngsters of all ages as they all pursue their dream of becoming a professional footballer. Heighway signed for the club as an amateur in 1970 after playing for Skelmersdale United and has a university degree. After winning numerous trophies at Anfield he returned to the club as the youth development officer in the 1980s, working alongside Roy Evans and leading Liverpool's youth team to their success in the FA Youth Cup in 1996. Having brought through talents such as Fowler, Gerrard, McManaman, Owen, Carragher, Matteo and Thompson, Steve was instrumental in setting up the world-leading Anfield Academy which opened on 20 January 1999.

HUGHIE McAULEY – UNDER-19 COACH

Joined the club as a schoolboy player and played professionally before moving on to play at Tranmere Rovers, Charlton Athletic, Plymouth Argyle and Carlisle. Hugh returned to Anfield in 1988 as Youth Coach. In June 1990, he moved in on a full-time basis and now coaches the Under-19s as well as working with the younger players. Hughie's hope is that at least three or four players each season can move from the Academy to the reserves and then maybe into the first team squad.

DAVE SHANNON – U-17 COACH

Dave has coached at the Centre of Excellence since 1988 and became full time when the Academy opened. Although he is primarily the U-17s coach he also has responsibility for the Under-14s, 15s, and 16s. He is so proud of every player who has progressed through the Liverpool youth ranks into the first team squad that he has a signed shirt from each of them at home. Dave played professional football for both Sunderland and Stockport County before working for the next 12 years on a part-time basis at Anfield. His Under-17s all left school in June 1999 after their GCSE's and completed their first year as full time footballers in 1999-2000.

FRANK SKELLY – OPERATIONS MANAGER

Frank has assumed various roles during his 25-year association with the club including scout, masseur, physiotherapist and coach. He first joined the club back in 1974 as a scout. He went onto coach the 'B' team and the Centre of Excellence before progressing to become the physiotherapist/masseur with the reserve side in 1992. Frank arranges the Academy fixtures for the Under-17 and Under-19 teams as well as the games for the younger boys, a minimum of ten matches every week. He is also responsible for the day-to-day running of the Academy including the 45-acre site with ten grass pitches.

SIMON FARNWORTH – PHYSIOTHERAPIST

Simon studied at Salford University before joining the club as a full time Senior Physiotherapist at the Academy in July 1998. Previous to this, Simon played professionally as a goalkeeper for Bolton Wanderers, Preston North End, Wigan Athletic and Bury.

BILLY STEWART – GOALKEEPING COACH

Billy is responsible for working with promising goalkeepers such as Peter Crookes and Matty Parry. He joined Liverpool in 1979 after playing for Liverpool boys but was released after two years and played League football with Wigan, Chester and Northampton (on loan) and Chesterfield, Southport and Hednesford Town.

TIM DEVINE – EDUCATION AND WELFARE OFFICER

Tim joined the Academy as the Head of Education and Welfare after 20 years in the teaching profession. He is responsible for arranging all aspects of education development and players' welfare needs. Tim helps with the 9-16 age group but spends most of his time with boys aged 17-21. The boys go to college for up to 12 hours a week where they can work towards a whole range of qualifications as well as a course skills programme to help the boys prepare for life as a professional footballer. This includes subjects like sports science and diet and nutrition.

under-19s

SATURDAY 28 AUGUST 1999

v HUDDERSFIELD TOWN (away) won: 5-2

Crookes, Cavanagh, O'Mara, Boardman, Jones, Navarro, Partridge 2, O'Brien (Porter), Armstrong 2, Miles, Olsen

Subs: Thompson, Grace, Culshaw, Torpey

SATURDAY 4 SEPTEMBER 1999

v MIDDLESBROUGH (home) won: 7-1

Crookes, Cavanagh, O'Mara, Boardman, Culshaw, Navarro, Thompson (Partridge), O'Brien Armstrong 6 (Jones), Miles, Olsen, (Torpey)

Subs: Parry

SATURDAY 11 SEPTEMBER 1999

v NEWCASTLE UNITED (home) lost: 0-4

Crookes, Cavanagh, Porter (O'Mara), Boardman, Jones, Navarro, Partridge (Thompson), O'Brien, Miles, Armstrong, Torpey (Olsen)

Sub: Hogg

SATURDAY 18 SEPTEMBER 1999

v SUNDERLAND (away) lost: 3-4

Crookes, Cavanagh, O'Mara, (Porter) Boardman, Jones, Navarro, Partridge, Park, Thompson 2, Miles, Olsen

Subs: Grace, Nicholas

SATURDAY 25 SEPTEMBER 1999

v LEEDS UNITED (away) won: 2-1

Crookes, Cavanagh, Porter, Boardman, Jones, Navarro, Partridge, Park, Thompson, Olsen, O'Mara

Subs: McIlroy, Parry, Whitbread

SATURDAY 16 OCTOBER 1999

v CREWE ALEXANDRA (away) drawn: 0-0

Crookes, Cavanagh, Olsen, Culshaw, Boardman, Navarro, Partridge, Park, Armstrong, Miles, Torpey (Thompson)

Subs: Grace, O'Mara, Jones, Whitbread

SATURDAY 30 OCTOBER 1999

v MANCHESTER CITY (home) lost: 0-2

Crookes, Cavanagh, Culshaw, Boardman, Porter, Partridge, Navarro, Park (Thompson), Olsen, Miles, Armstrong

Subs: Grace, Torpey, O'Mara

SATURDAY 6 NOVEMBER 1999

v MANCHESTER UNITED (away) drawn: 1-1

Crookes, Cavanagh, O'Mara, Boardman, Culshaw, Navarro, Partridge, Armstrong, Park, Miles, Torpey (Porter)

Subs: Hogg, Noel

SATURDAY 13 NOVEMBER 1999

v BLACKBURN ROVERS (home) lost: 0-3

Crookes, Cavanagh, O'Mara, Boardman, Culshaw, Navarro, Partridge, Park, Armstrong, Miles, Thompson

Subs: Torpey, Parry, Noel

SATURDAY 20 NOVEMBER 1999

v BOLTON WANDERERS (away) won: 2-0

Crookes, Cavanagh, O'Mara, Otsemobor, Culshaw, Navarro, Partridge, Olsen, Armstrong, Thompson, Torpey

Subs: Porter, Hogg, Noel

FRIDAY 26 NOVEMBER 1999

v EVERTON (away) won: 4-2

Crookes, Cavanagh, Culshaw, Boardman, O'Mara, Partridge, Navarro, Porter, Olsen, Armstrong (Thompson), Miles 2, Everton own goal

Subs: Parry, Porter, Torpey, Otsemobor

SATURDAY 4 DECEMBER 1999

v CREWE ALEXANDRA (home) won: 3-2

Crookes, Cavanagh, Porter, Culshaw, Boardman, Navarro, Partridge, Olsen, Thompson 2, Miles, O'Mara

Subs: Jones, Hogg, Noel

SATURDAY 11 DECEMBER 1999

v SHEFFIELD WEDNESDAY (away) won: 3-2

Crookes, Cavanagh, Porter, Boardman, Jones, Navarro, Partridge, Olsen, Thompson, Miles, O'Mara (Torpey)

Subs: Grace, Culshaw

FRIDAY 17 DECEMBER 1999

v EVERTON (home) lost: 0-1

Crookes, Cavanagh, Boardman, Jones, Porter (McIlroy), Partridge, Navarro, Park, O'Mara, Thompson, Torpey (Foley)

Subs: Otsemobor, Parry, Culshaw

SATURDAY 15 JANUARY 2000

v BARNSLEY (home) won: 4-0

Crookes, Cavanagh, O'Mara, Culshaw, Jones, Olsen, Thompson, **O'Brien,** Armstrong **(Porter),**
Miles **(Noel),** Torpey
Sub: Grace

SATURDAY 22 JANUARY 2000

v MANCHESTER UNITED (home) drawn: 1-1

Crookes, Cavanagh, O'Mara, Boardman, Jones, Navarro, Partridge, O'Brien (Thompson),
Armstrong, Miles, **Warnock (Olsen)**
Subs: Grace, Torpey, Culshaw

SATURDAY 19 FEBRUARY 2000

v STOKE CITY (home) won: 3-0

Crookes, Cavanagh, O'Mara (Porter), Boardman, Jones, Park, Thompson (Culshaw), O'Brien,
Miles 2, Armstrong, Olsen, Stoke City own goal
Subs: Parry, Warnock, Torpey

SATURDAY 26 FEBRUARY 2000

v COVENTRY CITY (home) won: 3-2

Crookes, Culshaw (Beck), Porter, Boardman, Jones, Park, Torpey **(Thompson), O'Brien,**
Armstrong, Miles, **Olsen**
Subs: Grace, Noel

SATURDAY 4 MARCH 2000

v NEWCASTLE UNITED (away) lost: 2-3

Crookes, Beck, Jones, Boardman, O'Mara, Thompson, O'Brien, Park, Olsen,
Armstrong 2, **Miles**
Subs: Porter, Hogg, Whitbread

SATURDAY 11 MARCH 2000

v MANCHESTER CITY (away) lost: 0-4

Crookes, Beck (Warnock), O'Mara, Boardman, Jones, Park, Thompson, O'Brien, Armstrong,
Miles, Olsen
Subs: Parry, Porter

SATURDAY 25 MARCH 2000

UNDER-19s PLAY-OFF

v WIMBLEDON (away) won: 4-3 after extra time

Crookes, Navarro, Warnock, Boardman, O'Mara, Partridge, Park, O'Brien (Foley),
Olsen (Thompson 2), Miles, **Armstrong**
Subs: Parry, McIlroy, Porter

v CREWE ALEXANDRA (away) lost: 1-2

Crookes, Navarro, O'Mara, Warnock, Boardman, Park (Foley), Partridge, O'Brien, Thompson, Miles, Olsen

Subs: Porter, Parry

UNDER-19s LEAGUE TABLE – GROUP B							
	P	W	D	L	F	A	Pts
BLACKBURN ROVERS	22	15	5	2	55	18	50
EVERTON	22	14	3	5	38	22	45
MANCHESTER UNITED	22	11	5	6	47	22	38
MANCHESTER CITY	22	12	2	8	45	32	38
LIVERPOOL	22	11	3	8	45	37	36
CREWE	22	7	8	7	29	34	29
BOLTON	25	3	3	16	18	55	12

FA Youth Cup

TUESDAY 30 NOVEMBER 1999

v WEST BROMWICH ALBION
3rd Round (away) won: 1-0

Crookes, Cavanagh, Porter (Beck), Otsemobor, Culshaw, Olsen, Thompson, Foley, Armstrong (McIlroy), Miles, Torpey

West Bromwich Albion own goal

Subs: Parry, Dawes

TUESDAY 25 JANUARY 2000

v NOTTINGHAM FOREST
4th Round (away) lost: 1-2

Crookes, Cavanagh, Otsemobor, Culshaw, Olsen, Thompson, O'Brien (Torpey), Foley (McIlroy), Warnock (Park), Miles, Armstrong

Subs: Porter, Parry

Under-18s Spanish Tournament – Easter 2000

FRIDAY 21 APRIL 2000

v REAL MADRID lost: 0-1

Crookes, Otsemobor, O'Brien, Warnock, Thompson, Olsen, Navarro, Porter, Miles, Armstrong, McIlroy

Subs: Beck, Parry, Coupe, Morton, Prince

SATURDAY 22 APRIL 2000

v ATHLETIC BILBAO won: 2-1

Parry, Otsemobor, O'Brien, Warnock, Thompson 2, Olsen, Navarro, Porter, Miles, Armstrong, McIlroy

Subs: Beck, Crookes, Coupe, Morton, Print

SUNDAY 23 APRIL 2000

v GUIPUZCOA lost: 0-1

Crookes, Otsemobor, O'Brien, Warnock, Thompson, Olsen (Coupe), Navarro (Beck), Porter (Prince), Miles, Armstrong (Morton), McIlroy

Subs: Parry

UNDER-19s SQUAD

Name	Birthdate	Position	Nationality
ARMSTRONG, Ian	16.11.81	Striker	English
BECK, Lee	06.09.82	Defender	English
BOARDMAN, John	06.09.80	Defender	English
CAVANAGH, Peter	14.10.81	Defender	English
CROOKES, Peter	07.05.82	Goalkeeper	English
CULSHAW, Paul	17.09.81	Defender	English
FOLEY, Michael	09.03.83	Midfield	Irish
JONES, Eifion	28.09.80	Defender	Welsh
O'BRIEN, Chris	13.01.82	Midfield	English
O'MARA, Paul	23.11.80	Defender	Irish
McILROY, Brian	12.10.82	Striker	English
MILES, John	28.09.81	Striker	English
NAVARRO, Alan	31.05.81	Midfield	English
OLSEN, James	23.10.81	Midfield	English
OTSEMOBOR, Jon	23.03.83	Defender	English
PARK, Stephen	03.10.81	Midfield	English
PARTRIDGE, Richie	12.09.80	Midfield	Irish
PORTER, Stephen	24.11.81	Defender	English
THOMPSON, Chris	07.02.82	Midfield	English
TORPEY, Stephen	16.09.81	Midfield	English
WARNOCK, Stephen	12.12.81	Midfield	English

NAME	APPS	GOALS	NAME	APPS	GOALS
ARMSTRONG, Ian	18	12	MILES, John	20	12
BECK, Lee	3	0	NAVARRO, Alan	17	2
BOARDMAN, John	22	0	NOEL, Leon	1	0
CAVANAGH, Peter	19	0	OLSEN, James	20	2
CROOKES, Peter	24	0	OTSEMOBOR, Jon	1	0
CULSHAW, Paul	12	0	PARK, Stephen	16	1
FOLEY, Michael	2	0	PARTRIDGE, Richie	17	5
JONES, Eifion	15	1	PORTER, Stephen	19	0
O'BRIEN, Chris	13	0	THOMPSON, Chris	20	9
O'MARA, Paul	20	2	TORPEY, Stephen	9	2
MCILROY, Brian	1	0	WARNOCK, Stephen	5	0

under-17s

SATURDAY 28 AUGUST 1999

v SHEFFIELD WEDNESDAY (home) won: 5-0

Hogg, Beck, Coupe, Otsemobor, McNulty, Morton, Peers (Noel), Foley 2, Mellor 2, McIlroy, Prince

Subs: Parry, Whitbread, Nicholas

SATURDAY 4 SEPTEMBER 1999

v MIDDLESBROUGH (home) lost: 0-1

Grace, Beck, Coupe, Otsemobor, McNulty, Fletcher, Morton (Peers), Foley, Mellor, McIlroy (Noel), Prince (Whitbread)

Subs: Welsh, Hogg

SATURDAY 11 SEPTEMBER 1999

v NEWCASTLE UNITED (home) won: 3-0

Parry, Beck, Coupe, Otsemobor, McNulty, Arnarsson, Peers, Foley, Mellor, McIlroy 2, Whitbread

Subs: Grace, Dawes, Welsh, Chambers

SATURDAY 18 SEPTEMBER 1999

v SUNDERLAND (away) lost: 1-5

Hogg, Chambers, Beck, Otsemobor, McNulty, Welsh, Peers (Dawes), Foley, Mellor, McIlroy, Whitbread

Subs: Parry, Murray, Smyth

SATURDAY 25 SEPTEMBER 1999

v LEEDS UNITED (away) lost: 0-3

Grace, Chambers (Welsh), Beck (Nicholas), Otsemobor, McNulty, Arnarsson, Prince, Foley, Mellor, Noel, Hackney

Subs: Dawes, Hogg

SATURDAY 2 OCTOBER 1999

v TOTTENHAM HOTSPUR (away) won: 4-0

Parry, Welsh, Beck, Otsemobor, McNulty, Arnarsson, Morton, Foley (Peers), Mellor 2, McIlroy (Dawes), Prince

Subs: Grace, Nicholas, Chambers

SATURDAY 16 OCTOBER 1999

v CREWE ALEXANDRA (away) lost: 2-7

Hogg, Beck, Nicholas, Otsemobor, McNulty, Morton, Peers (Noel), Foley, Mellor 2, McIlroy, Prince

Subs: Parry, Murray, Knowles

SATURDAY 30 OCTOBER 1999

v MANCHESTER CITY (home) won: 3-1

Parry, Beck (Connolly), Nicholas, Otsemobor, McNulty, Morton, Peers, Dawes, Prince, McIlroy 2, Whitbread

Subs: Hamilton, Harrison, Noel, Knowles

SATURDAY 6 NOVEMBER 1999

v MANCHESTER UNITED (away) drawn: 0-0

Parry, Beck, Nicholas, Otsemobor, McNulty, Dincer, Morton, Foley, McIlroy, Hamilton, Prince

Subs: Dawes, Grace, Peers Connolly, Butler

SATURDAY 13 NOVEMBER 1999

v BLACKBURN ROVERS (home) won: 2-1

Grace, Welsh, Beck, Otsemobor, McNulty, Dawes, Morton (Peers), Foley, McIlroy, Hamilton, Prince

Subs: Harrison, Nicholas, Connolly, Raven

SATURDAY 20 NOVEMBER 1999

v BOLTON WANDERERS (away) won: 1-0

Parry, Connolly, Beck, Welsh, McNulty, Dawes, Smythe, Foley, McIlroy, Murray, Prince (Whitbread)

Subs: Wright, Grace, Raven, Butler

TUESDAY 23 NOVEMBER 1999

v LEEDS UNITED (home) won: 2-0

Hogg (Parry), Connolly, Beck, Welsh (Raven), McNulty, Dawes 2, Smyth (Murray), Foley, Noel, McIlroy, Whitbread

Subs: Butler, Wright

SATURDAY 4 DECEMBER 1999

v CREWE ALEXANDRA (home) won: 3-2

Grace, Connolly (Butler), Beck, Raven, McNulty, Dawes, Peers, Foley, Murray, McIlroy, Whitbread

Subs: Kenna, Harrison, Power, Wright

SATURDAY 11 DECEMBER 1999

v SHEFFIELD WEDNESDAY (away) won: 2-1

Parry, Raven, Beck, Otsemobor, McNulty, Dawes (Peers), Morton, Foley, Noel (Murray), McIlroy 2, Whitbread

Subs: Connolly, Hogg, Butler

v BARNSLEY (home) lost: 0-3

Hogg, Chambers (Connolly), Beck, Otsemobor, McNulty, Dawes, Peers, Martin, Murray (Smyth), McIlroy, Whitbread

Subs: Parry, Raven, Noel

v MANCHESTER UNITED (home) lost: 1-2

Parry, Beck, Coupe, Otsemobor, McNulty, Dawes, Morton, Foley, Noel (Smyth), McIlroy (Murray), Whitbread (Nicholas)

Subs: Hogg, Chambers

v BLACKBURN (away) lost: 0-1

Hogg, Beck, Nicholas, Otsemobor, McNulty, Dawes, Morton, Foley (Whitbread), Noel (Murray), McIlroy, Coupe

Subs: Chambers, Parry, Peers, Connolly

v BOLTON WANDERERS (home) won: 4-0

Parry, Beck, Nicholas, Otsemobor, McNulty, Kristjansson, Morton, Foley, Prince 2, McIlroy, Coupe

Subs: Dawes, Harrison, Whitbread, Smyth, Chambers

v BARNSLEY (away) won: 5-1

Grace, Beck, Coupe, Otsemobor, McNulty, Morton, Dawes (Peers), Foley, Noel (Whitbread), McIlroy 2, Prince

Subs: Hogg, Chambers, Murray

v COVENTRY CITY (home) drawn: 1-1

Hogg, Chambers, Coupe, Otsemobor, McNulty, Morton, Dawes, Peers (Whitbread), Smyth, McIlroy, Prince

Subs: Parry, Raven, Vaughan

v NEWCASTLE UNITED (away) won: 2-1

Parry, Welsh, Nicholas, Otsemobor, McNulty (Chambers), Morton, Dawes, Foley, Noel, McIlroy, Coupe (Peers), Newcastle United own goal

Subs: Grace, Smyth, Murray

SATURDAY 11 MARCH 2000

v MANCHESTER CITY (away) lost: 0-2

Grace, Welsh, Nicholas, Otsemobor, McNulty, Morton, Dawes, Foley (Chambers), Noel (Murray), McIlroy, Thomas (Smyth)

Subs: Hogg, Raven

TUESDAY 21 MARCH 2000

**UNDER-17s ACADEMY
LEAGUE PLAY-OFF**

v COVENTRY CITY (away) lost: 1-5

Parry, Beck (Dawes), Coupe, Otsemobor, McNulty, Morton, Welsh, Foley, Prince, McIlroy, Whitbread (Peers)

Subs: Nicholas, Noel

UNDER 17s LEAGUE TABLE – GROUP B

	P	W	D	L	F	A	Pts
CREWE	22	13	3	6	74	35	42
MANCHESTER UNITED	22	13	2	7	59	29	41
BLACKBURN ROVERS	22	11	5	6	43	34	38
LIVERPOOL	22	12	2	8	41	32	38
MANCHESTER CITY	22	11	2	9	42	25	35
BOLTON	23	3	1	18	19	61	10

Under-17s Italian Tournament

v VENEZIA drawn: 1-1

Parry, Chambers, Nicholas, Whitbread, McNulty, Welsh, Peers, Dawes, Noel, Murray, Thomas (Smyth)

Subs: Harrison, Vaughan, Wright, Raven, Butler, Gillespie

v VICENZA lost: 1-2

Parry, Chambers, Nicholas, Whitbread, McNulty, Welsh, Peers, Dawes, Noel (Raven), Murray, Thomas (Smyth)

Subs: Mannix, Vaughan, Butler, Wright, Harrison

v CHIEVO VR won: 4-1

Parry (Harrison), Chambers, McNulty, Raven, Nicholas, Noel, Welsh 2 , Dawes, Peers, Murray (Wright), Smyth

Subs: Butler, Mannix, Gillespie

UNDER-17s SQUAD

Name	Birthdate	Position	Nationality	Name	Birthdate	Position	Nationality
ARNARSSON, Viktor	22.01.83	Midfield	Iceland	McNULTY, Stephen	26.09.83	Defender	English
BECK, Lee	06.09.82	Defender	English	MELLOR, Neil	04.11.82	Forward	English
BUTLER, Chris	18.10.84	Defender	English	MORTON, Anthony	28.01.83	Midfield	English
CHAMBERS, David	13.08.84	Defender	English	MURRAY, Matthew	08.09.84	Forward	English
CONNOLLY, Paul	24.08.84	Defender	English	NICHOLAS, Andrew	10.10.83	Defender	English
COUPE, Alan	13.10.82	Defender	English	NOEL, Leon	10.01.84	Forward	English
DAWES, Ian	16.03.84	Midfield	English	OTSEMOBOR, Jon	23.03.83	Defender	English
DINCER, Fatih	13.07.83	Midfield	Turkish	PARRY, Matty	30.03.83	Goalkeeper	Welsh
FLETCHER, Darren	01.02.84	Midfield	Scottish	PEERS, Mark	14.05.84	Forward	English
FOLEY, Michael	09.03.83	Midfield	Irish	PRINCE, Neil	17.03.83	Midfield	English
GRACE, Stephen	07.09.82	Goalkeeper	English	RAVEN, David	10.03.85	Defender	English
HACKNEY, Simon	05.02.84	Forward	English	SMYTH, Mark	09.01.83	Forward	English
HAMILTON, Mark	22.03.84	Forward	Irish	THOMAS, Mark	09.01.85	Forward	Welsh
HOGG, Matthew	13.09.82	Goalkeeper	English	WELSH, John	10.01.84	Defender	English
KRISTJANSSON, Sigmunder	09.09.83	Midfield	Iceland	WHITBREAD, Zak	04.03.84	Defender	English
McILROY, Brian	12.10.82	Forward	English				

NAME	APPS	GOALS	NAME	APPS	GOALS
ARNARSSON, Viktor	3	0	McNULTY, Stephen	23	2
BECK, Lee	20	0	MELLOR, Neil	7	7
BUTLER, Chris	1	0	MORTON, Anthony	17	1
CHAMBERS, David	5	0	MURRAY, Matthew	8	0
CONNOLLY, Paul	5	0	NICHOLAS, Andrew	9	0
COUPE, Alan	10	1	NOEL, Leon	11	1
DAWES, Ian	16	6	OTSEMOBOR, Jon	20	0
DINCER, Fatih	1	0	PARRY, Matty	11	0
FLETCHER, Darren	1	0	PEERS, Mark	14	2
FOLEY, Michael	20	2	PRINCE, Neil	13	3
GRACE, Stephen	6	0	RAVEN, David	3	0
HACKNEY, Stephen	1	0	SMYTH, Mark	5	0
HAMILTON, Mark	2	0	THOMAS, Mark	1	0
HOGG, Matthew	7	0	WELSH, John	9	0
KRISTJANSSON, Sigmundur	1	0	WHITBREAD, Zak	14	0
McILROY, Brian	22	16			

trip to china

'BEHIND THE BAMBOO CURTAIN'

Liverpool, who have been champions of Europe more times than any other British club, broke new ground on another continent when their Under-19 team played two matches in China as ambassadors for their country and their city.

The invitation for the Anfield club to make the 6,000-mile trip behind the 'Bamboo Curtain' came as part of the city of Liverpool's twinning celebrations with Shanghai during October 1999. Together with Liverpool's Lord Mayor, Councillor Joe Devaney and other political, civic and academic representatives a party of 17 players travelled, accompanied by five members of the Anfield staff. They comprised Chief Executive Rick Parry, Football Academy Director Steve Heighway, Under-19 coach Hughie McAuley, physiotherapist Simon Farnworth and Education and Welfare Officer Tim Devine.

The verdict of all concerned was that the landmark trip was a huge success on and off the field, despite the fact that Liverpool narrowly lost both their games. 'There's a tremendous amount going in football in China and you genuinely feel they're at the start of something there which is very, very exciting' said Rick Parry. Both Liverpool's games were screened live on Chinese TV and British viewers were kept on the ball by Granada TV who travelled with the Liverpool party to make a special documentary entitled 'Reds In China', fronted by reporter Andy Gill, who recalled: 'The Liverpool team played and trained in conditions far different from anything they had previously experienced and in a culture as far removed from life at the Academy as you could find. But the visit was also a chance for the Liverpool coaching staff to tell their Chinese counterparts how they are developing our young players.' Football's popularity is growing rapidly in China, whose professional league was launched only six years ago. The Liverpool visitors held coaching clinics and it was agreed that two boys from Shanghai would visit the Liverpool Academy for a month.

'While we were there we took the opportunity to pass on to the Chinese the Liverpool way of doing things,' said Steve Heighway. 'We have a history, culture and a tradition in the way we play our football. They were interested in finding out our ways of coaching young people and playing the game. Ours is a simple philosophy of a talented individual playing for the team and realising the importance of teamwork and the concept of team, plus a simplistic belief in pass and move.' In meetings with Chinese football officials and coaches Steve outlined the various age categories and principles of the Liverpool youth programme. He told them: 'Up to ten years old we call the age of fun and enjoyment, from 10 to 12 we call the age of technique, from 12 to 14 the age of understanding and from 14 to 16 the age of competition. We want the boys to be competitive. We also think speed is very important. Even with the young players we do some work on speed but it's always speed with the football.' Steve's colleague Hughie McAuley said: 'Rick Parry, Steve Heighway and myself had a meeting with the Chinese FA where we discussed the development of football at youth level. We also talked to the

Chinese coaches about how our youth programme at Liverpool works. Tim Devine played a big role out there, as well. He gave the lads some interesting talks on different cultures and ways of life.'

Liverpool's opening game was against Shenwai at a stadium outside Shanghai and Hughie reported: ' It was pleasing that we created many opportunities. We missed a lot of chances in the first half and unfortunately fell behind after the break. Despite the fact that we continued to carve out scoring opportunities we couldn't get the equaliser. That was a disappointment but it was a good opening match and, in general, we were pleased with our performance. We should have been more clinical in front of goal and, on another day, we would have won the match quite comfortably.'

The second game, against a Shanghai FA XI, was played on a Saturday evening at the city's new Hongkou Stadium, the first in China to be purpose built for football. 'On the morning of the game we invited youngsters from a Chinese orphanage to join in our training session,' added Hughie. 'They really enjoyed themselves, which was great to see. The match was well promoted and it was great to see a big crowd, consisting mainly of youngsters who were very enthusiastic in their support. Again, we played well in perfect conditions and it was no surprise when we took the lead.

'Chris Thompson and John Miles created the opening and Ian Armstrong did well to round the goalkeeper and score. A defensive slip let them in for an equaliser, which was disappointing. Because there were a couple of trophies up for grabs it was decided we would settle the match on penalties. Unfortunately, we lost 6-5. For the record, our successful penalty takers were Peter Cavanagh, Ian Armstrong, John Miles, Alan Navarro and Paul O'Mara.' Hughie summed up thus: 'We should have won both our games but the lads played some good football and, at the end of the day, we couldn't have asked for any more. I think the lads enjoyed themselves and it was a once-in-a-lifetime experience for them.' Steve Heighway reflected: 'Just the experience of going to China is part of the maturing process for young players… and you can't give them too many maturing experiences.'

THURSDAY 21 OCTOBER 1999

v SHENWAI lost: 0-1

Crookes, Cavanagh, Culshaw, Boardman, O'Mara, Partridge, Park, Miles, Navarro, Torpey, Thompson

Subs: Prince, Porter, Parry, Armstrong, Jones, Olsen

SATURDAY 21 OCTOBER 1999

v SHANGHAI FA XI drawn: 1-1 lost 6-5 on penalties

Crookes, Cavanagh, Culshaw, Boardman, O'Mara, Partridge, Navarro, Olsen, Thompson, Armstrong, Miles

Subs: Park, Parry, Porter, Prince, Jones, Torpey

europe
2000-2001

LIVERPOOL CONTINUE ANFIELD'S EUROPEAN ODYSSEY

There was applause far beyond Merseyside and the legions of Kop fans when Liverpool booked their ticket back into Europe via the UEFA Cup because there is something lacking in the flavour of Continental competition when the Anfield club are not involved. Despite recent lean years Liverpool are England's most successful European standard bearers since they first entered the old-style European Cup back in August 1964.

Their four European Cup triumphs – 1977, 1978, 1981 and 1984 – have been supplemented by two UEFA Cup wins, in 1973 and 1976, when the final was played on a two-leg home and away basis, and a Super Cup victory in 1977.

So Liverpool will be seeking a record UEFA Cup hat trick in their 2000-2001 campaign when their first outing in Europe will be the club's 180th game in the various tournaments.

'To qualify for the UEFA Cup with two games of last season still to go was an achievement in itself,' said manager Gerard Houllier. 'The previous year we finished with nothing so it shows how much we have improved and we are all looking forward to competing in Europe.'

Liverpool's last two European ventures have been in the UEFA Cup. In 1998-99 they were eliminated in the third round by Celta Vigo and the previous season went out to Strasbourg in round two. Their next challenge could be another testing one because they will be joined in their English record 28th European campaign by many of Europe's big names including Benfica, Ajax, Roma, Bordeaux, Fiorentina, Celtic and Nantes.

Postal Applications

Tickets for **HOME** FA Premier League matches may be purchased, **as available**, 26 days in advance of the match. Applications by post should clearly state the match required and must include a stamped addressed envelope together with the correct remittance. Cheques or Postal Orders should be made payable to Liverpool Football Club. Applicants wishing to pay by credit or debit card must give details of their card number and expiry date. Debit card applications must also include the issue number. In the event that the number of applications received for the first day of sales exceeds the number of match tickets available, a ballot system will be administrated. Postal applications should be addressed to:-

LFC Ticket Office, PO Box 204, LIVERPOOL, L69 4PQ

Telephone Bookings

Tickets for **HOME** FA Premier League matches to a maximum of four may be purchased, **as available**, 26 days in advance of the match by telephoning 0151 263 5727 and quoting your credit or debit card number and expiry date. A minimum of 50 pence per ticket will be charged. Tickets booked within three days prior to the match will be forwarded by post. Tickets booked after this period will have to be collected from the Ticket Office at the credit card collections window and the card used for the bookings must be produced for inspection at this time.

Personal Applications

Tickets for all **HOME** Premier League matches may be purchased, **as available**, from the Ticket Office 19 days in advance of the match. Recent history has shown that for the majority of Premier League fixtures the available match tickets have been sold via postal and telephone bookings, and that no tickets have been available within the nineteen day period for personal applications.

A voucher system will apply in respect of the home FA Premier League matches against Everton and Manchester United.

	Reserved Seat Prices – Match Tickets	
	Category A	Category B
Main Stand Centenary Stand Paddock Enclosure Anfield Road	£26.00	£23.00
Combined Anfield Road Adult Child 1 Adult/1 Child	£39.00	£34.50
Kop Grandstand	£24.00	£21.00
Kop Grandstand Adult Child 1 Adult/1 Child	£36.00	£31.50

Category A Matches: Everton, Manchester United, Newcastle United, Arsenal, Tottenham Hotspur, Leeds United, Chelsea, Aston Villa, Sunderland, Manchester City

The concessionary rate for children is applicable to children aged 16 and under.

Please note for adult/child combined tickets a ratio of two adults to one child or two children to one adult is allowed. In the event that the number of children exceed the ratio of 2:1 the additional tickets will be charged at the adult rate.

Away Matches

Tickets for domestic away matches initially go on sale to Liverpool Football Club season ticket holders, subject to the selling arrangements announced. In the event that the full allocation of tickets are not taken up by season ticket holders, details of a general sale will be made. In the event of a GENERAL SALE, tickets can be purchased either by post, by sending the correct remittance and a STAMPED ADDRESSED ENVELOPE, or by ringing the Telephone Credit Card Line, a minimum booking fee of 90p per ticket will be charged. Please note that credit card bookings can only be accepted in the event of a general sale and bookings being made three days prior to the match.

Domestic and European Fixtures

Ticket information concerning the F A Cup, Worthington Cup and UEFA Cup allocations will be made as soon as possible after each draw has taken place and the venues are known.

Ticket Office Hours

Monday-Friday	**9.15 a.m. to 4.45 p.m.**
Match Days **(Saturday and Mid-week)**	**9.15 a.m. to kick-off, then** **15 minutes after end of game**

Non-match Saturdays Closed

24 Hour Ticket Information Line
0151 260 9999

Supporters are advised that they should retain all their ticket stubs as these may be used on any additional fixtures allocated on a voucher system or in the event of a fixture which has to be abandoned at Anfield.

LIVERPOOL FOOTBALL CLUB RESERVE THE RIGHT TO CHANGE ANY OF THE ABOVE SELLING ARRANGEMENTS OR MATCH CATEGORIES WITHOUT PRIOR NOTICE

supporters' clubs

It may come as a surprise that despite Liverpool's amazing success over the years and their worldwide following, there has never been an 'official' supporters' club for the vast number of fans who live all over the UK and the World. So May 1992 saw the launch of the 'LIVERPOOL FOOTBALL CLUB INTERNATIONAL SUPPORTERS' CLUB' run by Liverpool and its staff from their Anfield Stadium, and which now boasts a membership in excess of 50,000 that is increasing daily. Aimed at uniting fans worldwide, detailing team performances and 'inside' goings on at the club, but most importantly enabling them to voice their views and become a vital part of the world's greatest football club!

The International Supporters' Club can be contacted at:

Liverpool FC ISC, PO Box 205, Anfield Road, Liverpool, L69 4PS

Tel: 0151 261 1444   Fax: 0151 261 1695

England

AMBLESIDE, KENDAL & DIST
- GRAHAM TYSON, MARKET PLACE, AMBLESIDE, CUMBRIA, LA22 9BU,

BRISTOL
- PAUL WAIT, 64 HILLSIDE ROAD, ST GEORGE, BRISTOL, BS5 7PA,

CAMBRIDGE
- MARTIN COOPER, 189 COOLIDGE GARDENS, COTTENHAM, CAMBS, CB4 4RH

CARLISLE
- MARK SLEIGHTHOLM, 29 HERON DRIVE, KINGFISHER PARK, CARLISLE, CA1 2WA

CHESTERFIELD
- MARK HEALEY, 12 WRENPARK ROAD, WINGERWORTH, CHESTERFIELD, S42 6RZ

CORBY
- DAVID WALPOLE, 9 CHAPEL STREET, TITCHMARSH, KETTERING, NORTHANTS, NN14 3DA

CORNWALL
- STEVE BAWDEN, P.O.BOX 81, TRURO, CORNWALL, TR1 3YX

COVENTRY
- KEVIN HOLLOWAY, 15 HORNINGHOLD CLOSE, ERNSFORD GRANGE, COVENTRY, CV3 2GH

DONCASTER
- STEVE MAXWELL, 14 OLDFIELD LANE, STAINFORTH, DONCASTER, DN7 5ND

EAST ANGLIAN
- JAMES SHREEVE, 15 FEN GREEN CLOSE, OULTON BROAD, LOWESTOFT, SUFFOLK, NR32 3QW

ESSEX
- MRS PAT WOOLER, P.O. BOX 2684, CHELMSFORD, ESSEX, CM2 8FG

EAST CLEVELAND
- HARRY HOWES, 2 VALLEY AVENUE, LOFTUS, SALTBURN, CLEVELAND, TS13 4SD

EAST YORKSHIRE
- DAVE SMITH, 190 STEYNBURG STREET, HULL, HU9 2PG

GUERNSEY
- ANDY PRIAULX, MARCHEZ DESSUS, RUE A CHIENS, ST SAMPSONS, GUERNSEY, GY2 4AD

HULL
- MARK CALVERT, 61 GREYGARTH CLOSE, NORTH BRANSHOLME, HULL, HU7 5AP

ISLE OF MAN
- MIKE GORDON, MOUNTVIEW, TYNWALD ROAD, PEEL, ISLE OF MAN, IM2 1JP

KENT
- STEVE GILL, 47 MARSHALL STREET, FOLKESTONE, KENT, CT19 6ES

JERSEY
- PAUL ASHTON, 21 RUE DE LE JARDIN DE LA HAUTEUR, MONT AU PRETRE, ST HELIER, JE2 4NY, JERSEY

LEEDS
- NORRIE BRENNAN, 1 GREEN LANE, LEEDS, LS11 7EZ

LEICESTER
- STUART FRIBBENS, 13 PARRY STREET, LEICESTER, LE5 3NL

LONDON
- MATTHEW SELBY, P O BOX 185, LONDON, NW1 3QU, (+s.a.e.)

MERSEYSIDE
- LES LAWSON, 23 WINDSOR VIEW, LODGE LANE, LIVERPOOL, L8 0UN

MILTON KEYNES
- DOLLY WALLINGER, 2 BOUVERIE WALK, NORTHAMPTON, NN1 5SP

NEWCASTLE
- KEITH JELLEY, 46 EASTBOURNE GARDENS, WALKERDENE, NEWCASTLE ON TYNE, NE6 4DY

NOTTINGHAM
- MICK STEVENS, 65 NEWHOLM DRIVE, SILVERDALE, WILFORD, NOTTINGHAM, NG11 7FR

PLYMOUTH
- DUNCAN HEDGES, 184 CLITTAFORD ROAD, SOUTHWAY, PLYMOUTH, PL6 6DJ

PRESTON
- ROB WOODHOUSE, 3 INSKIP ROAD, LEYLAND, PRESTON, PR5 3JJ

SCARBOROUGH
- JOHN HUGHES, 6 MOUNT PARK AVENUE, SCARBOROUGH, YO12 5HE

SHROPSHIRE/IRONBRIDGE
- DAVE WESTHEAD, LLANERCH COTTAGE, HYSSINGTON, CHURCH STOKE, MONTGOMERY, POWYS, SY15 6DZ

SHROPSHIRE/SHREWSBURY
- STEVE ASHFORD, 11 HUNTERS COURT, HUNTER STREET, MOUNTFIELDS, SHREWSBURY, SY3 8QN

STAFFORD
- ANDREA BASKERVILLE, 11 ST LUKES CLOSE, NORTON BRIDGE, STONE, ST15 0PD

STOKE
- ANDRE PETROVIC, 15 FIRST AVENUE, KIDSGROVE, STOKE ON TRENT, STAFFS, ST7 1DN

THAMES VALLEY
- EDDIE SMART, 20 SEDGEMOOR, FARNBOROUGH, HANTS, GU14 8JN

THANET
- KEVIN HENRICH, 38 HELENA AVENUE, MARGATE, KENT, CT9 5SL

TIVERTON
- GRAHAM FROST, 33 HEATHCOAT WAY, TIVERTON, DEVON, EX16 6TR

TRENT VALLEY
- VENA GENT, 20 ASHTREE BANK, BRERETON, RUGELEY, STAFFS

WORCESTER
- NOREEN DANIEL, , 15 CORNMEADOW GREEN, CLAINES, WORCESTER, WR3 7PN

Wales

CARDIFF
- MANDY EDWARDS, 4 REDWOOD DRIVE, CHANDLERS REACH, LLANTWIT, FARDRE, CARDIFF, CF38 2PG

GWENT
- STEVE CAIN, 100 CHEPSTOW ROAD, MAINDEE, NEWPORT, GWENT, NP19 8EE

GWYNEDD
- DAVID ROBERTS, BRYN MEURIG, CARMEL, CAERNARFON, GWYNEDD, LL54 7DS

JONES LLANFAETHLU
- COLIN AVERY, BRYN TIRION ISAF, LLANFAETHLU, HOLYHEAD, ANGLESEY, LL65 4NL

WEST WALES
- PHIL PARDOE, 65 HEOL REHOBOTH, FIVE ROADS, LLANELLI, SA15 5DZ

Northern Ireland

BALLYMENA
- JAMES McCLOY, 64 GORTAHAR ROAD, RASHARKIN, BALLYMENA, CO ANTRIM, BT44 8SB

BROADWAY
- JOE McCAFFREY, 36 MOYARD PARK, BELFAST, BT12 7FS

CASTLEROCK
- RICHARD STEEN, 52 DRUMARD DRIVE, COLERAINE, CO LONDONDERRY, BT51 3EX

COLERAINE
- ANDY MAGUIRE, 18 LOGUESTOWN PARK, COLERAINE, CO DERRY, BT52 2HR

COOKSTOWN
- NOEL McFETRIDGE, 54 CASTLE VILLAS, COOKSTOWN, CO TYRONE, BT80 8JE

COMBER
- PAUL McBRIDE, 22 DALTON GLEN, COMBER, CO. DOWN, BT23 5RJ

CRUMLIN
- SIMON MOORE, 8 CAIRN WALK, CRUMLIN, CO ANTRIM, BT29 4XA

DROMORE
• MALCOLM RUSSELL, 13 WILLOW DRIVE, BANBRIDGE, CO DOWN, BT32 4RF

DUNGANNON
• RONNIE COWAN, 17 KILLYNEILL COURT, DUNGANNON, CO TYRONE, BT71 6BN

FIRST ARDOYNE
• MICHAEL FLYNN, 29 DUNEDEN PARK, BELFAST, BT14 7NE

FIRST BANGOR
• TREVOR OSBORNE, 60 ORANGEFIELD AVENUE, BELFAST, BT5 6DH

FIRST DERRY
• MARTIN CASSIDY, 47 CROMORE GARDENS, CREGGAN ESTATE, DERRY BT48 9TF

FIRST LARNE
• DON DODDS, 10 BAY PARK, LARNE, CO ANTRIM, BT40 1BZ

IRVINESTOWN
• ALAN KEYS, DRUMADRAVEY, LISNARICH, IRVINESTOWN, CO FERMANAGH, BT94 1LQ

KILROOT
• ROBERT CRAWFORD, 23 QUEENSWAY, CARRICKFERGUS, CO ANTRIM, BT38 7LA

LIMAVADY
• HELSBY HOUSTON, 47 DERNAFLAW ROAD, DUNGIVEN, CO LONDONDERRY, BT47 4PR

NEWRY
• MALACHY MCMAHON, 80 PARKHEAD CRESCENT, NEWRY, CO DOWN, BT35 8PE

PORTAFERRY
• IAN SMITH, 91 HIGH STREET, PORTAFERRY, NEWTOWNARDS, BT22 1QU

RATHCOOLE
• JOHN McCORD, 24 OLD IRISH HIGHWAY, RATHCOOLE, NEWTOWNABBEY, CO ANTRIM, BT37 9LG

SEVEN TOWERS
• TREVOR KYLE, 19 FARM LODGE AVENUE, BALLYMENA, CO ANTRIM, BT43 7DF

SILVERSTREAM
• GEORGE GREENHILL, 32 SILVERSTREAM AVENUE, BELFAST , BT14 8GQ

SION MILLS
• ANTHONY COOKE, 33 SYCAMORE AVENUE, SION MILLS, CO TYRONE, BT82 9HT

SLIABH DUBH
• HUGH FITZSIMMONS, 26 COLINVIEW STREET, SPRINGFIELD ROAD, BELFAST, BT12 7EN

SOUTH ANTRIM
• JOE LYNN, 12 ARDFERN PARK, SAUL ROAD, DOWNPATRICK, BT30 6XZ

WARRENPOINT
• JIM O'CONNOR, 7 AVOCA LAWNS, WARRENPOINT, NEWRY, CO DOWN, BT34 3RJ

WEST BELFAST
• LARRY CLAXTON, 123 MOYARD CRESCENT, BELFAST , BT12 7HL

Eire

CAVAN
• JOHN JOE GAVIN, CLINAGORE, CLONES, CO CAVAN

CLARE
• BARRY O'KEEFE, DRUMCLIFF ROAD, ENNIS, CO CLARE,

CORK
• JOHN O'CALLAGHAN, ROCKSPRING, LISCARROLL, MALLOW, CO CORK
• JOHN O'SULLIVAN, 31 TIFFANY DOWNS, BISHOPSTOWN, CO CORK,
• CHARLIE ANKETTELL, GNEEVES, BOHERBUE, MALLOW, CO CORK
• FIONA BARRY, 11 WOLFE TONE PARK, FERMOY, CO CORK

DONEGAL
• EAMONN MCNELIS, DERRIES, GLENTIES, CO. DONEGAL
• KENNETH KEE, CORCULLION, CASTLEFIN, CO DONEGAL
• KEVIN NEELY, 1 CELTIC PARK AVENUE, WHITEHALL, DUBLIN 9
• JOSEPH MCLAUGHLIN, MONTAY'S, BRIDGE STREET, CARNDONAGH, CO DONEGAL

DUBLIN
• TOM DEVOY, 15 TARA COVE, BALBRIGGAN, CO DUBLIN
• CATHERINE BRADY, 15 HUNTSDOWN ROAD, MULHUDDART, DUBLIN 15
• TOM BEATTY, 20 GLENVIEW PARK, TALLAGHT, DUBLIN
• COLM McAULEY, 28 ABBEYWOOD CRESCENT, LUCAN, CO DUBLIN
• DECLAN GREAVES, 36 WOODAVENS, CLONDALKIN, DUBLIN 22

GALWAY
• PAUL HEHIR, 51 GAELCARRAIG PARK, NEWCASTLE, GALWAY

KERRY
• LEO BYRNE, 97 BALLOONAGH EST, TRALEE, CO KERRY
• DECLAN CARTY, 5 DIRHA EAST, LISTOWEL, CO KERRY

LAOISE
• TOM GORRY, 8 PATTISON ESTATE, MOUNTMELLICK, CO LAOISE

LIMERICK
• PAT DEERE, 13 WILLIAM STREET, LIMERICK, IRELAND
• DERMOT HORAN (SOUTH LIMERICK), STONE PARK, BRUFF, CO LIMERICK

LONGFORD
• TONY KILKENNY, KILCURRY, BALLYMAHON, CO LONGFORD

LOUTH
• RICHARD SULLIVAN, KILPATRICK, ARDEE, CO LOUTH
• LORNA MCQUILLAN, 128 PEARSE PARK, DROGHEDA , CO LOUTH
• CIARAN O'CONNOR, 155 CEDARWOOD PARK, DUNDALK, CO LOUTH

MAYO
• DAVID RYDER, 37 HORKANS HILL, WESTPORT, CO MAYO
• MARTIN GLYNN, 118 GREENHILLS ESTATE, BALLINA, CO MAYO

MONAGHAN
• MARTINA KENNEDY, LOUGHMOURNE POST OFFICE, CASTLEBLAYNEY, MONAGHAN

ROSCOMMON
• EDWARD CONROY, 55 FOREST VIEW, BOYLE, CO ROSCOMMON

SLIGO
• EAMONN McMUNN, "OCEAN VIEW", BELTRA, CO SLIGO

TIPPERARY
• T.J. LOOBY, 20 ST BERNADETTE TERRACE, OLD BRIDGE, CLONMEL, CO. TIPPERARY

WATERFORD
• DECLAN POWER, 74 ARD NA GREINE, WATERFORD

WESTMEATH
• SEAN O'BEIRNE, 104 MEADOWBROOK, ATHLONE, CO WESTMEATH
• TONY COLLINS, 46 GINNELL TERRACE, MULLINGAR, CO WESTMEATH

WEXFORD
• JOHN HOWLIN, BALLINABLAKE, CURRACLOE, ENNISCORTHY

Europe and Rest of the World

BELGIUM
• PETER BRUYNSEELS, VALLEISTRAAT 16, 2222 WIEKEVORST, BELGIUM

CYPRUS
• SIMOS SAKKA, TRITONOS 2, LARNACA 6047, CYPRUS

DENMARK
• PER KNUDSEN, MELHOLTVEJ 10, 9220 AALBORG EAST, DENMARK

GERMANY
• PHIL MCNALLY, HAUPSTRASSE 33, 6144 ZWINGENBERG 2, RODAU, GERMANY

GIBRALTAR
• JULIAN SENE, 32 DURBAN COURT, HARBOUR VIEWS, GIBRALTAR

GREECE
• THOMAS PAPANIKOLAOU, LFC ISC HELLENIC BRANCH, P.O. BOX 34111, ATHENS 10029, GREECE

HONG KONG
• PHILIP CHU, C/O FIGURE HEADS, ROOM 1022, STAR HOUSE, TSIMSHATSUI, HONG KONG

ICELAND
• EVERT EVERTSSON, P.O. BOX 409, ALFHOLSVEG 127, KOPAVOGI, ICELAND 202

JAPAN
• KEIKO HIRANO, TAISHIDO 1-4-35-903, SETAGAYA-KU, TOKYO 154, JAPAN

MALAYSIA
• DR FATAH, YAYASAN FAS, BANGUNAN YAYASAN FAS, 554, 47301 KELANA JAYA, SELANGOR, MALAYSIA
• KAHAR KASIM, B1 SELANGOR PROPERTIES, UKAY HEIGHTS, AMPANG 6800, SELANGOR, MALAYSIA

MALTA
• MATTHEW PACE, GOLDEN HARVEST, NAXXAR ROAD, SAN GWANN, SGN 08, MALTA

MAURITIUS
• JEAN CARL PALMYRE, MORRISON STREET, PAMPLEMOUSSES, MAURITIUS

NORWAY
• PAUL MOLLER, FINSTADSLETTA 133, N-1475 FINSTADJORDET, NORWAY

SINGAPORE
• HENRY MINJOOT, BLK 46 LOR. 5, TOA PAYOH, #07-97 310046, SINGAPORE

SWEDEN
• JAN-OVE JOHANSSON, ALSTIGEN 7, HEDEMORA 77634, SWEDEN

SWITZERLAND
• OFFICIAL SWISS BRANCH, P.O. BOX 596, CH-2501 BIEL-BIENNE, SWITZERLAND

SOUTH AFRICA
• DAN TANNE, P.O. BOX 890783, LYNDHURST 2106, SOUTH AFRICA

U.S.A.
• HANK EDWARDS, P.O. BOX 7071, FDR STATION, NEW YORK, NY 10150, U.S.A.,